The Impact of the Russian Revolution on Britain

Robin Page Arnot

Published in 2017 by Manifesto Press Cooperative Limited
© 1967 Robin Page Arnot
Originally published in 1967 by Lawrence & Wishart

This edition transcribed by Martin Levy and republished by permission of
Robin Page Arnot's literary executors

ISBN 978-1-907464-30-0.

Typeset in Bodoni and Gill
Printed in Britain by Russell Press

Robin Page Arnot: a biography

Robin Page Arnot was born on 15 December 1890 at Greenock, where his father was the editor of the *Greenock Telegraph* and *Clyde Shipping Gazette*. He studied at Glasgow University, where he helped to form the University Socialist Federation in 1912, with G D H Cole and others, and of which he was to become its chair. He contributed to the Independent Labour Party's *Labour Leader*, under the *nom de plume* of Jack Cade.

He was closely connected with the Labour Research Department from its beginnings. In 1912 the Fabian, Beatrice Webb, had established a committee of enquiry into "the control of industry in the state of tomorrow". One of the volunteers attracted to the project was Arnot. The committee soon turned into the Fabian Research Department and in 1914 Arnot became its full-time secretary, a post he held until 1926.

Arnot was called up to fight in the war in 1916. He refused to go, being opposed to war, and was imprisoned for two years in Wakefield as a conscientious objector. When he was released in 1918 he returned to his former post as secretary of the Fabian Research Department, which had by then changed its name to the Labour Research Department, having become an independent "fact-finding body for the trade union and labour movement".

In 1919 the miners demanded higher wages, shorter hours and nationalisation of the mines. The government established a Committee of Enquiry, and the Miners' Federation asked the LRD for help. Arnot assembled evidence on their behalf and publicised the miners' cause. Arnot, together with H H Slesser, the Federation's legal advisor, drafted the Mines Nationalisation Bill which was presented to the Royal Commission set up by the government. During the railway strike later that year, Arnot and the LRD organised publicity for the railwaymen. Arnot also wrote a history of the LRD in 1926.

Along with a number of others, such as Walter Holmes and William Mellor, who dubbed themselves the "Guild Communist Group", a left trend amongst a larger movement for 'guild socialism', Arnot was one of the founder members of the Communist Party of Great Britain (CPGB) in 1920. His strong intervention in the debate about Labour Party affiliation, for which he was in favour, marked him out as an advocate of British Communism's fixing itself firmly as part of the wider labour movement.

With R Palme Dutt and W N Ewer, Arnot set up the Trinity Trust that formed *Labour Monthly*, which ran from 1926 to 1981 and was long edited by Dutt. In all that time, Arnot was a regular contributor and working editor for the journal. From October 1922, he was one of a three-man commission that worked for a year on measures to reorganise the British Communist Party. He also became a member of the Party's Central Committee and as such was arrested under the 1797 Incitement to Mutiny Act in 1925, in the run up to the General Strike, and spent six months in jail. He was released on the eve of the strike and helped to form the Northumberland and Durham Joint Strike Committee. He later returned to the LRD as Director of Research and wrote a book on the general strike.

Arnot was a British representative at the 6th Congress of the Communist International in 1928 and was the first Principal of the Marx Memorial Library from 1933 until the end of the Second World War. He was elected to the LRD's Executive in 1938 and was re-elected every year until 1976, when he was made Honorary President. He died in 1986 aged 96, from 1984 publicly and openly fighting the revisionist trend that was taking control of the CPGB, even to the end.

(From http://www.grahamstevenson.me.uk/)

Publications by Robin Page Arnot:

Labour Research Department:
Facts from the Coal Commission, not dated [1919].
The Russian Revolution: A Narrative and a Guide for Reading, 1923.
The Politics of Oil: An Example of Imperialist Monopoly, 1924.
The General Strike, May 1926: Its Origin and History, 1926.
The General Strike and the Miners' Struggle, 1926.
History of the Labour Research Department, 1926.

Communist Party of Great Britain:
Fight the Slave Plan: The Dawes Plan Exposed, not dated [c 1924].
How Britain Rules India, 1929.
Slavery or Socialism, not dated [c 1934].
Fascist Agents Exposed in the Moscow Trials, 1938.
What is Common Wealth?, 1943.
May Day 1945.

George Allen & Unwin:
Trade Unionism on the Railways: Its History and Problems. With G D H Cole, 1917.
Further Facts from the Coal Commission: Being a History of the Second Stage of the Coal Industry Commission, with Excerpts from the Evidence, not dated [1919].
A History of the Miners' Federation of Great Britain:
Vol 1: The Miners, 1949.
Vol 2: The Miners: Years of Struggle, 1953.
Vol 3: The Miners in Crisis and War, 1961.
Vol 4: One Union, One Industry, 1979.
A History of the Scottish Miners, 1955.

South Wales Miners – Glowyr de Cymru: A History of the South Wales Miners' Federation, Vol 1 (1898-1914), 1967.

Martin Lawrence/Lawrence & Wishart:
William Morris: A Vindication, ML, 1934.
Twenty Years: The Policy of the Communist Party of Great Britain from its Foundation, July 31st, 1920, L&W, 1940.
The Impact of the Russian Revolution in Britain, L&W, 1967.

Labour Monthly:
Japan, not dated [c 1942].
There Are No Aryans, not dated [1943] *(Australian edition: Current Book Distributors, Sydney*, 1944).

Other:
Nationalisation of the Mines, not credited or dated, *Daily Herald* [1919].
Soviet Russia and Her Neighbors. With Jerome Davis, Vanguard Press, New York, 1927.
A Short History of the Russian Revolution from 1905 to the Present Day, 2 vols, Victor Gollancz, London, 1937.
Soviet Leaders: Stalin, Current Book Distributors, Sydney, not dated [1942].
1917-1942: From Tsardom to Soviet Power, Russia Today Society, London, 1942.
Japan: Strength and Weaknesses, Trinity Trust, London, 1942.
Bernard Shaw and William Morris: A Lecture, given on May 11, 1956, William Morris Society, London, 1957.
South Wales Miners – Glowyr de Cymru: A History of the South Wales Miners' Federation, Vol 2 (1914-1926), Cymric Federation Press, Cardiff, 1975.

Editorial note

This book, originally published in 1967 in connection with the 50th anniversary of the Russian Revolution, is being republished to coincide with the Centenary of that event. Manifesto Press is very grateful to the heirs and literary executors of Robin Page Arnot, who hold the copyright, for permission to undertake this republication. In transcribing the original text, for the benefit of today's readership, minor changes to punctuation and a small number of typographical corrections have been made, and some additional notes have been added where citations or explanations appeared necessary. Despite having made rigorous checks, it remains possible that the text presented here will include a few transcription errors, for which apologies are offered. We hope that the reader will overlook such oversights in view of the value of the narrative once again being presented.

Martin Levy
October 2017

Preface

The calendar worked out by Sosigenes under the auspices of Julius Caesar over two thousand years ago (and retained in Britain until 1752) was still in use in Russia up to the Spring of 1918. Thus Russia was behind our dating by thirteen days till these disappeared in February 1918, whose fourteenth day followed directly upon its first day. In my narrative, I have throughout described everything in terms of our new style calendar. Thus the Revolution that overthrew the Tsardom (and here dated March 12) occurred on February 27 in the Julian Calendar and has hence been termed "The February Revolution". Similarly "The October Revolution" was dated as October 25 and 26, but actually took place in our new style on November 7 and 8. As far as possible I have used the more modern transliterations, eg Tsar and not Czar, Mendeliev and not Mendelieff, as was the spelling current in Britain fifty years ago and still, to my ear, more expressive of the sounds of these Russian consonants.

Zelda Kahan, singled out for commendation by Lenin in 1911 for her anti-jingo standpoint within the British Social-Democratic Party, was later responsible with her husband the late W P Coates for a series of volumes on this subject, and so has put me under an obligation which I take the opportunity of this preface to acknowledge.

Transcripts of Crown-copyright records in the Public Record office appear by permission of the Controller of HM Stationery Office.

R Page Arnot
April 23, 1967

Contents

Chapter 4   The Making of Peace

Chapter 5   Intervention – 1918

Chapter 5   Intervention – 1919

Chapter 7   Intervention – 1920

❚ The First Stage

❙ Rough winds of March

On the sixteenth day of March 1917, when some ten million or more morning papers were seen by the population of Great Britain, the readers beheld the almost universal headlines: "Abdication of the Tsar" and "Revolution in Russia". The news came like a bolt from the blue for most of the population. It was for them as unexpected and as unpredictable as a devastating earthquake, an eruption of Vesuvius or of Hekla. But this social earthquake, unlike the convulsions of nature, where interest in places that are remote from the scene of events lasts only for days, was a continuing wonder and cause of excitement, of emotional fears and hopes and finally of irrational apprehensions and hatreds. It was not a nine days wonder nor nine weeks, for the Revolution in Russia, thus begun and thus announced, continued month by month to its climax some two hundred and forty days later.

Owing to the war-time censorship, little could get through to the public that was not authorised by the naval and military censors; but in this case it was a double censorship. There was the censorship in Tsarist Russia, there was the censorship also in Britain. Consequently news did not leak out but came all in one burst, like the bursting of a great dam as when a lake high in the Pamirs or in the Andes or in New Zealand bursts through and devastates everything. Such a devastating piece of news was the abdication of the Tsar with all its consequences in what was immediately recognised to be the Russian Revolution. It was the first stage of the Revolution. There were more and greater events to come, with an impact that was to be deeper and wider and with effects that last to this day.

Actually, in spite of the censorship in Russia, certain happenings had appeared, such as the assassination on the last day of December 1916 of Rasputin by members of the Russian Royal Family. Here some inkling of what had occurred was given or could not be concealed. Murder will out, as Macbeth said. It crossed the censorship also in Britain. But there was at this time a third censorship exercised by certain newspaper proprietors, the abiding censorship of the owners of the millionaire press. In the case of *The Times*, the leading press organ in Britain, it was decided to say little or nothing about the assassination of Rasputin. Equally little was said about the reports given by Lord Milner, a member of the War Cabinet who had gone to Russia to estimate the situation. It was generally understood that Lord Milner, reaching Russia at the end of January for a Conference of Allies on the conduct of the war and leaving before the beginning of March, had brought back the report that "there was no danger of revolution".

Earlier in that month of March 1917, however, there had been some rumours. There was the rumour on March 4 of grave riots in Petrograd, following on a failure in the ration system. This news was repeated on the 12th in the British papers. It did not cause the same stir as it would have done in 1914 or 1915, for already the British people were feeling the shortage of food: bread was tending to be short and potatoes, the main substitute, were to prove in short supply. The sinkings that spring of 1917 by the German submarines of ships carrying grain to the shores of Britain had already acquainted the population with the possible danger of famine arising from war conditions. That the same sort of danger was being encountered in Russia did not seem necessarily to presage popular rising or revolutions.

It was in the mid-March of 1917 that the British people found in their newspapers that the Tsar of Russia had abdicated and that a provisional government, made up of some members of the Duma, was likely to be formed. It was learned at the same time that there were councils of workers' delegates in being; and that the abdication of the Tsar had occurred or had been raised as early as March 12, which in future was regarded as the single day when it could be said the first stage of the Russian Revolution began. Censorship with its non-release of news meant that newspaper offices throughout the world were not told the facts until evening on March 15, late upon the Ides of March. That day, not only in Europe, but throughout North America, throughout Asia, in the newspapers of Japan, Australia and Mexico, and even in the newspapers of Shanghai where the Chinese Government had that month been brought into the war on the side of the Allies, the information of this, the Red Portent, was simultaneously and universally communicated.

No previous revolution had such a simultaneous spread of its news, nowhere and at no time in history had there been such a simultaneous impact of a great world-shaking event. The American Revolution of 1776, the French Revolution of 1789, the English Revolution of 1640 onwards had all spread by means of couriers, letters, messages, carried on horseback, carried by ship, carried by men on foot, men on camels, men on every kind of cattle and vehicle. Never until 1917 was it possible, with the invention some half to three-quarters of a century before of the electric telegraph, for such news to come simultaneously to every part of the world. Consequently the impact of the Russian Revolution was rendered a million-fold greater than any other by its effect on so many hundreds of millions of people at one and the same time.

The Allies, the public of Britain and the British Empire were particularly interested. It is with the impact upon them that this book is concerned. But on the same day on the continent in the Swiss town of Zurich there were a number of Russian exiles. Amongst them was Vladimir Ilych Ulyanov, known then and since by his revolutionary name of Lenin. He too on the Ides of March heard of the Revolution that had begun its first stage earlier that week; and immediately began thinking out ways and means for the exiles to get back into Russia, to which in the meantime he wrote his instructive *Letters From Afar*.

2   The impact on Fleet Street

Whatever happened in war-torn Europe and was passed by the multiple censorship of the belligerents (apart from the private or secret communications to governments or to other authorities and influential persons) was conveyed almost entirely through the newspaper press. The telegrams might be held up or suppressed. But it was fairly certain that nothing except tenuous rumours could spread in comparison with the stentorian announcements coming from the printing machines of the press and, above all, of the 'national newspapers' of London's Fleet Street – the dozen that contained general news.[1] In the second rank, but in the area of their circulation even more authoritative than the Fleet Street papers, were such morning dailies as the *Yorkshire Post, Yorkshire Observer, The Scotsman* of Edinburgh, the *Glasgow Herald* and *The Western Mail* of Cardiff. Besides these there were many hundreds of local papers, often the sole journals read by their purchasers.

In all of the Fleet Street papers there were only three morning papers that were Liberal and two evening papers, the *Westminster Gazette* and the *Star*. There were no Labour papers existing as at that time: it was not till two years later that there came into existence the *Daily Herald*.[2]

Every paper had been keeping silence for the simple reason that no telegrams had been reaching them from Russia in that second week of March 1917, apart from rumours of the food riots in Petrograd.

Preceded on the evening of March 15 by announcements in Parliament, the newspapers on the morning of Friday March 16 were seen with uniform headlines beneath which a flood of pent-up telegrams ran throughout their columns on page after page. *The Times*, then owned by the millionaire Lord Northcliffe, led off with "Revolution in Russia" and "Abdication of the Tsar". The *Manchester Guardian* similarly on its page 4 had "Revolution in Russia" and on page 5 "Tsar Abdicates". The *Daily Telegraph* headlines were "Revolution in Russia" and "Abdication of the Tsar: Regent Appointed: the Duma's Coup – Ministers Arrested" and then across five columns "Abdication of the Tsar". The *Morning Post* was similar. The *Daily Chronicle* on its front page had the banner headline "Successful Revolution in Russia" and beneath that "Abdication of the Tsar". All Fleet Street for once in its long career had a unique similarity in headlines; and so too had the provincial press. The only variations were in spelling, the *Daily Mail* and the *Daily Express* preferring to use the Polish version "Czar". Beneath these headlines ran the news in detail, some of it sufficiently accurate, some of it the product of wishful thinking on the part of those who fed the British correspondents with tit-bits of 'news'. Then came the editorials of which we may select the following:

The Times, which had as its first heading "Revolution in Russia – A 'Win the War' Movement", had on its middle page the editorial "The Russian Revolution":

"A great Revolution has been accomplished in Russia. After nearly a week of chaos in Petrograd something like a parliamentary government controls the situation. The Tsar has abdicated in favour of his infant son, and his brother, the reforming Grand Duke Michael, is expected to act as Regent. The news will hardly come as a surprise to those acquainted with the internal situation in the Allied Empire as it has recently developed, and who have observed the ominous suspension of telegrams from Russia within the last few days." *(16.iii.1917)*

Beneath the main heading "Abdication of the Tsar" on column three of the leader page the headings were "First News from Petrograd – Revolution Complete – Army and Duma Combine – Rapid Restoration of Order – the New Regent". On the next day (Saturday) further telegrams were run. The editorial was "The Situation in Russia", the lead-in was still "Abdication of the Tsar" and there was a brief reference to "Labour Party's Message".³

The *Manchester Guardian* carried a glowing editorial on Friday March 16 describing the Revolution as the "deadliest blow to the war *morale* of Germany". The influence this editorial had in British ruling circles is discussed in Section 6, 'Is it Dual Power?'

The *Daily Chronicle*, Friday March 16, beneath a seven-column banner on the "Successful Revolution in Russia", carried double-column headlines: "Abdication of the Tsar – His Brother Grand Duke Michael as Regent – Duma, People, Army and Navy against Pro-Germans – First Object of New Duma Government: To Win the War." On the same page on columns three and four there ran "Collapse of the Old Regime – Cabinet Arrested". On columns six and seven M G Farbman, London correspondent of the *Bourse Gazette* of Petrograd, writes: "How the Throne Tried to Forestall the People – Reaction in Russia Plays its Last Card – and Loses. Revolution provoked by the Court Camarilla" and refers to "Protopopov's Plan to Provoke a Crash" and, with the Cossacks ready, then to "Start the Blood-Letting". The editorial on page 2 ran "Long Live Russia" and dealt with the overthrow of the "Dark Forces" There was a box with the following:

VIVE LA DUMA

"The Duma will revive in one form or another. We can say with all sincerity, 'The Duma is dead, long live the Duma'." These memorable words spoken in French were addressed by the late Sir Henry Campbell-Bannerman on 23rd July, 1906, to the Congress of the Inter-Parliamentary Union held in London. The Duma had been dissolved by Imperial decree. This week's Revolution followed a similar decree dissolving the Duma.

The *Daily News*, which from its ownership by the extremely rich Cadbury family was often dubbed 'the Cocoa Press', in a leader on Friday March 16 had a seven-column banner "Abdication of the Tsar" and then on columns one and two

"Revolution in Russia. Duma Forms New Government and Arrests the Cabinet. Troops Join the People."

The *Morning Post*, chiefly owned by Countess Bathurst, on Friday March 16, on page 4, column three, in an editorial headed "Russia a Nation" stated that German "emissaries and agents" had poured "poison into the ear of the Emperor Nicholas himself and strove to persuade him that the dynasty was threatened by the cause of the Allies"; that German agents "had the Prime Minister Stuermer in their pay"; and lastly they referred to Rasputin and compared what had happened to the glorious revolution of 1688 and the downfall of King James II. On Saturday March 17, after a first editorial on Russia headed "What Does it Mean?", a second editorial on "Russia and Germany" said: "One result of the Revolution in Russia will be to make the Russian Army more formidable to Germany than ever before."

In the *Daily Express*, owned by the millionaire Lord Beaverbrook, the headlines additional to the common headline of "Abdication of the Czar – Revolution in Russia" ran "Parliament in Control of the Empire: Czar's brother as Regent". On page 2, on the fifth column, it was stated "The Czar is a nephew of Queen Alexandra and the Czarina whom he married in 1894 was the daughter of the Grand Duchess of Hesse (Princess Alice of Great Britain). Both Czar and Czarina are therefore first cousins to King George." *(16.iii.1917)*

The *Daily Mail* (also in Lord Northcliffe's combine) on March 16, on page 4, columns two and three, had an editorial headed "Great Events in Russia. Why the Czar Abdicated" and referring to some of these "great events", stated:

"The most tremendous of all is the 'benign revolution' which has taken place with all the suddenness of an earthquake in Russia. From Monday until last night the cables have been silent. In the interval vast changes have been accomplished as by some cosmic cataclysm. A Provisional Government appointed by the Duma is in possession after a fierce conflict with the reactionaries. The battle is over. The German plotters in Petrograd have sustained the most signal defeat. The cause of freedom and the allies has triumphed." *(16.iii.1917)*

Thereafter the *Daily Mail* quotes at length "our Correspondent H Hamilton Fyfe on 1st February", whose article had the headlines "The Rebirth of Russia. Why Rasputin was killed. The Czar's Opportunity", and said that "Rasputin was one of the tools of German intrigue." On page 5 of the *Daily Mail* (of that Friday March 16) there ran a seven-column banner "Abdication of the Czar" and below it headlines "Great Events in Russia. Complete overthrow of German Influence".

Such was the impact of the news from Petrograd upon the Fleet Street morning newspapers; such, too, was their immediate comment. From Left-wing Liberal to ultra-Right Conservative, all agreed in judging the Revolution from the standpoint of Britain's interest in the war. Like true English empirics they put the happenings in Russia to the test: if it helps to win the war against German imperialism, revolution is a good thing; if it does not, then it is a bad thing. How this initial standpoint remained or developed or altered and disintegrated is the story of the press in the year 1917.

What had actually happened that month after a winter of strikes and disturbances in the capital city of Russia can be conveniently put here in tabular form as a diary of events in Petrograd.

DIARY OF EVENTS

March

3   Beginning of strike at Putilov Plant in Petrograd (corresponding to Woolwich Arsenal); Martial Law proclaimed.

7   With food shortage continuing, women in queues raid bakers' shops.

8   International Women's Day: demonstration (at the call of the Petrograd Bolshevik Committee) of working women and housewives, against hunger, war and Tsardom; strikers join in.

9   Strike of 200,000 against Tsardom and war despite police bans and barriers.

10 300,000 come out in General Strike: clashes with armed police; red banners bear slogans "Down with the Tsar!", "Down with the War!", "We want bread!" From the Army headquarters Tsar Nicholas to General Khabalov: "I command you to put a stop to the disorders in the capital not later than tomorrow."

11 The strike becomes a rising: police shoot down demonstrators in Znamenskaya Square. Solders called out to quell riots open fire instead on mounted police. Women and factory workers fraternise with soldiers.

12 *Morning:* factory workers disarm police; soldiers of Guards Regiment refuse to fire on demonstrators, join workers in revolt and then bring out soldiers from other barracks to the number of 66,000. Workers are supplied by soldiers with small arms in scores of thousands.

  Afternoon: call from hasty meeting of socialist, trade union and co-operative officials for delegates from factories and regiments to form Petrograd Soviet or Council.

  Evening 10 pm: formation and inaugural meeting of Petrograd Soviet of delegates; Executive Committee chosen. The Tsardom is overthrown.

13 Petrograd Soviet meeting with over a thousand delegates adopts Order No 1, taking control of all armed forces, giving the men civilian rights and abolishing officers' privileges. Tsar's ministers are arrested. Leaders of various landlord and capitalist parties set up "Provisional Committee of the State Drama to re-establish order", including one newly declared "Socialist-Revolutionary".

14 Tsar Nicholas signs the deed of abdication. His brother the Grand Duke

Michael declines the offer of succession. At the request of the leaders of the Petrograd Soviet the "Provisional Committee" becomes the "Provisional Government".

15 *Evening:* news of the Revolution in Russia and of the abdication is released to the world press.

16 Impact of the Russian Revolution in its first stage conveyed in the newspapers to hundreds of millions throughout the world.

3 Impact on the weeklies

The Sunday newspapers followed a path similar to the dailies, both in treatment of news and in comment. For example *The Observer*, founded 1791, put it that:

> "An example is given to the Kaiser's subjects – political slaves now by comparison with emancipated Russia – which will shake to its foundations the German governing system which caused the war … The triumph won by the Duma and the Army together for freedom and modern government is one of the greatest and best things of time. The breath of a new morning is felt not only by Russia but by all mankind." *(18.iii.1917)*

The Nation, a Left-wing Liberal organ edited by the one-time Fabian, H W Massingham, opened with a paean of praise:

> "The greatest tyranny in the world has fallen. The glorious news of the successful Russian Revolution will send a thrill of joy through democratic Europe."

It goes on in its London Diary:

> "Liberalism has won its first great victory on the moral battleground where all along the true conflict was going on. … Association with the Tsar was a curse and an incubus. Alliance with the Russian people is a glory." *(17.iii.1917)*

So much for the immediate impact on the weeklies, one Independent Conservative and one Liberal. Others followed suit, more or less. It was much the same with the socialist weekly journals, from the Fabian *New Statesman* to *The Labour Leader*, organ of the Independent Labour Party, the *Herald* edited by George Lansbury, *The Clarion* edited by Robert Blatchford, *Justice* controlled by H M Hyndman. There was also the Glasgow Forward, which proclaimed the March events to be a "Whig revolution"; the *Women's Dreadnought*, edited by Sylvia Pankhurst; *The Socialist*, appearing irregularly as the organ of the Socialist Labour Party; and *The Call*, the organ of the British Socialist Party.

A particular interest attaches to this last periodical, which had been founded nearly a twelve-month earlier as an organ of international socialism. It had supported broadly the international socialist conference of anti-war sections, first at Zimmerwald on September 5-7, 1915, and then at Kienthal on April 27-30, 1916, when the resolutions passed were not only for peace but for revolutionary socialism. But neither the British Socialist Party nor the much larger Independent Labour Party were allowed passports to attend these conferences.

In *The Call* the Russian socialist groups in Britain found a harbourage and their contributions appeared not infrequently in its columns. Consequently it had a closer connection with Russia and with Russian exiles than most other socialist weeklies.[4]

4 The impact on parliament

Simultaneously with the release to the press of the telegrams, the news from Petrograd and the official response to the news was given in Parliament. Late at night on Thursday March 15, 1917, the House of Commons was told that for nearly a week (since "Friday night last") it had been known that there was "serious trouble in Russia". "Only tonight," stated the Leader of the House, Bonar Law, "a message was received from our Ambassador to the effect that a telegram had been received from the Duma announcing that the Tsar had abdicated and that the Grand Duke Michael Alexandrovitch had been appointed Regent." There was also a comfort ("and a real comfort") that "all our information leads us to believe that the movement is not in any sense directed towards an effort to secure peace, but, on the contrary". Four days later, on Monday, Prime Minister Lloyd George, having said that he could not as yet give a "detailed account of what has actually occurred", made the following statement:

"There has for some time been deep discontent in Russia, of which there have been several manifestations, due to the inefficiency of the Government in the conduct of the War. On Friday, the 9th, some riots, due to the scarcity of food, occurred in the streets of Petrograd. This was, however, the occasion rather than the cause of the Revolution which immediately followed.

"The soldiers who were commanded to take action against the rioters refused to obey orders, and gave their support to a committee, of which the President of the Duma was the head, which had been suddenly formed for the purpose of preserving order, and the control of the Government passed largely into the hands of this committee. Subsequently a strong Provisional Government was formed, of which Prince Lwoff is the head, and the Proclamation of this Government, as well as that of the Tsar announcing his abdication for himself and his son, and that of the Grand Duke Michael, have appeared in the Press, and also the refusal of the latter, while placing his services at the disposal of the new Government, to accept the throne unless called to it by the voice of the people, expressed in a constituent assembly." *(19.iii.1917)*

Lloyd George, who found it "satisfactory" that the new Government "has been formed for the express purpose of carrying on the war with increased vigour", concluded on behalf of the government with confidence that:

> "these events, marking as they do an epoch in the world and the first great triumph of the principle for which we entered the war, will result, not in any confusion or slackening in the conduct of the war, but in the even closer and more effective co-operation between the Russian people and its Allies in the cause of human freedom".

Thus at the very outset the Members of Parliament were given a one-sided picture of "one of the landmarks in the history of the world"; but it corresponded to what they wished to believe and hoped would happen. Later that week similar sentiments were uttered in debate upon a resolution, set down by Lloyd George, as follows:

> "That this House sends to the Duma its fraternal greetings and tenders to the Russian people its heartiest congratulations upon the establishment among them of free institutions in full confidence that they will lead not only to the rapid and happy progress of the Russian nation but to the prosecution with renewed steadfastness and vigour of the war against the stronghold of an autocratic militarism which threatens the liberty of Europe." *(22.iii.1917)*

Chancellor of the Exchequer Bonar Law in his opening said:

> "What has happened in Russia reminds us of the earlier days of the French Revolution. We recall with what a glow of hope the fall of the Bastille was received by liberal-minded men throughout the world, a feeling which was thus expressed by our own poet:

> 'Bliss was it in that dawn to be alive,
> But to be young was very heaven!'

> "We recall, too, how quickly and how sadly that bright dawn was overcast. It is too soon to say that all danger is over in Russia. It is too soon to feel confident that the new Government has already laid the foundation on which, in the words of Burke, liberty 'will have wisdom and justice for her companions, and will lead prosperity and plenty in her train'."

It was remarked by radical journalists, not without a grain of malice, how words of welcome to a revolution came ill that Thursday from the Tory leader, who stumbled in his quotation from the poet and seemed happier to bask in sentiments drawn from the venal Burke. Bonar Law concluded that "the Mother of Parliaments" should send friendly greetings to "the Parliament of an Allied country", saying:

> "It is not too soon for us to send a message of good will to the new Government, a Government which has been formed with the declared intention of carrying this war to a successful conclusion, and a Government which has undertaken a task as arduous as has ever fallen to the lot of any administration – the task at once of driving out a foreign aggressor and of establishing freedom and order at home." *(22.iii.1917)*

The leader of the Conservative Party was followed by the official spokesmen of each of the other parties, ex-Premier Asquith for the Liberals, Devlin for the Irish Nationalists, and Wardle for the Labour Members, each of them rejoicing in the downfall of autocracy and claiming to welcome Russia "into the fellowship of free peoples". For them this first stage of the Revolution was a triumph of liberal institutions and a very present help in trouble to the British in their war effort.

Such, in the press and in Parliament, was the first impact of the first stage.

5 The impact on the Labour movement

The first impact of the Russian Revolution was that an upward heave was given to Labour which suddenly became important and which also began to feel itself more important. The rulers of Britain realised that the presence of Labour in the coalition might be even more useful than before in carrying out the purposes of Government which were channelled into the successful prosecution of the war. In mid-December Arthur Henderson had been made one of the War Cabinet of 5; now the importance of the Labour element in the Government was greatly increased both from the standpoint of friend and foe. What had previously been a necessity to be accepted, namely that the 40 Labour Members out of a total elected lower house of 670 members, or one-sixteenth of the whole assembly, must be given places and posts in war-time because the interest they represented was far more important than was suggested by their numbers, was now welcomed. Labour, renovated and refurbished, had become a positive asset in dealing with their Russian ally. For it was clear that, all of a sudden, a prominent part would henceforth be played by those who claimed to represent the interests of the 'lower classes' of Russia, the working class and the peasants. Hence, the moment the news of the Revolution reached London, every facility and publicity was given to the despatch of a telegram signed by 20 leading figures, 14 being Members of Parliament, including 6 holding Government office, headed by the Labour member of the War Cabinet, Arthur Henderson. Amongst them also were the chief officers of the Parliamentary Labour Party and its National Executive Committee, and leaders of the biggest trade unions.[5]

The *Morning Post*, under the heading "British Labour Leaders. Message of Sympathy and Exhortation", gave the text of the telegram sent "to MM Kerensky and Chkheidze, the leaders of the Russian Labour Party", *viz:*

"Organised Labour in Great Britain is watching with deepest sympathy the efforts of the Russian people to deliver themselves from power of reactionary elements which are impeding their advances to victory. Labour in this country and France has long realised that despotism of Germany must be overthrown if way is to be opened for free and peaceful development of European nations.

"This conviction has inspired them to make unprecedented efforts and sacrifices, and we confidently look forward to assistance of Russian Labour in achieving the object to which we have devoted ourselves.

"Earnestly trust you will impress on your followers that any remission of effort means disaster to comrades in trenches and to our common hopes of social regeneration." *(17.iii.1917)*

Previously it had been necessary for the British Government to have ambassadors and emissaries and envoys that would fit in with the preoccupations of the Tsar and his court ministers. Hence the despatch in January 1917 of Lord Milner, one of the 5 of the War Cabinet, to try and pull things together and reach a good arrangement with their ally. It had been necessary to propitiate the Tsar: it was now necessary to propitiate the Soviet. This was a new feature far more to be reckoned with than the Provisional Government which owed its existence so largely to Allied help and recognition. Therefore those who viewed with growing apprehension and doubt the proceedings of the Petrograd Soviet were at the same time anxious to make a display of friendliness towards it. Hence, after March 16, before a month was out, two veterans of the Labour movement (and of the old socialist movement before there was a Labour Party) were approved by the War Cabinet as a delegation to go to Petrograd where it was hoped that their presence would demonstrate solidarity between the peoples of the British Empire and the Russian Empire.

The two envoys were chosen with some care. They were: Will Thorne, MP from 1906, Member of the Parliamentary Committee of the Trades Union Congress from 1894, one of the founders of the National Union of General Workers in the late '80s when he had quite a close personal acquaintance with Frederick Engels and, according to the story, was helped to improve his powers of reading and writing by no other than Eleanor Marx, youngest daughter of Karl Marx; and James O'Grady MP, born 1866, who had been one of the founders similarly of a trade union, the National Union of Distributive Workers, and was regarded as one of the outstanding socialists in the Labour Party. It may be added that when they got to Petrograd the fact that these two were strong supporters of the Lloyd George Government and of 'the fight to a finish', somewhat impaired the effect that had been hoped for from their long membership of the Labour movement, from their working-class origin, and from their position as leading trade union officials.

Meanwhile, apart from the official welcome given by all parties in the House of Commons on the motion put forward by the government, and apart from all the proffered friendliness, the impact on the Labour movement began to show itself amongst the rank and file. A rousing welcome was given to the Russian Revolution in every working-class organisation. After all, the Labour movement had been supporters of the movement of the socialist parties and of the peoples of the Tsarist Empire in opposition to the Tsardom. This had dated from the 19th century, a heritage from the First International. It had been the frequent subject of early socialist meetings and demonstrations. The hatred towards the Tsar and the Tsar's Government as an oppressive reactionary power was widespread. The attitude was shown in such a detail as the popular name for the mounted police in London who were used to control demonstrations: they were called "The Cossacks", a term of opprobrium which dated from before Bloody Sunday of November 1887.

Consequently after the new happenings in Russia, meetings and demonstrations began to be held in increasing numbers. On March 31, 1917 a great meeting was held in the Albert Hall, London's largest hall of assemblage with a capacity of over 12,000. The meeting was called "To Welcome The Russian Revolution".

From this moment onwards the Labour movement as a whole and the socialist societies in particular were coming out in favour of the Russian Revolution. But there was a difference. Most of the Labour Party, like all of the Tories and like nearly all the Liberals, hoped that the Revolution would result in a further prosecution of the war, whereas a small minority amongst the Liberals and in each section and affiliated organisation of the Labour Party hoped fervently that the Revolution would further the cause of early peace, peace by negotiation, peace without annexations and without indemnities. This last was particularly felt and voiced by the socialist societies which had taken up a standpoint in accordance with the 1912 Basle Manifesto of the International Socialist Congress.

This latter standpoint was represented by *The Labour Leader*, the organ of the Independent Labour Party; by *The Call*, founded in February 1916, the organ of the British Socialist Party; and by a few other intermittently appearing papers, such as *The Socialist*, organ of the Socialist Labour Party, centred mainly on the Clyde, and *The Woman's Dreadnought*, which soon was to take on the title of *Workers' Dreadnought*, organ of the Workers' Suffrage Federation, directed by Sylvia Pankhurst. In addition there was the *Herald*, edited by George Lansbury.

There were also less popular papers (published at a higher price) such as the *New Statesman* and *The Nation*, which occasionally contained articles critical of the mainly pro-war trend of these journals.

Beyond these were socialist papers which had completely abandoned the standpoint put forward at three consecutive International Socialist Congresses, namely: *Justice*, founded in 1884, and now given over to jingoism; *The Clarion*, founded in the early '90s; and lastly *The New Age*, editor A R Orage with S G Hobson as a regular contributor.[6]

6 Is it dual power?

Before the summer months, indeed before the end of April 1917, the glad, confident welcome from Britain's press and Parliament began to be accompanied by much questioning. The news from Russia each week brought both hopes and fears to the rulers of an empire who were aware (as their public were not) of the extensive mutinies in the French armies, and of the very many months that would pass before the new belligerent, the United States, would be capable of playing a significant part in the armed conflict. Hopes and fears – each brought an array of questions.

Was the dissolved Duma, by its constitution so unrepresentative of the mass of the people, really a firm foundation on which to construct a new and effective cabinet of ministers? Or had it been a mere simulacrum of a Parliament, in which a motley of dissentient landlords and urban capitalists reserved to themselves all but one sixth of the seats? In any case, it had not the power of the purse or power over ministerial policy. From such powerlessness, could a powerful Government be born and thrive amid the rigours of revolution? Had it indeed any sure backing beyond the ready recognition of Entente embassies?

There began in Britain to be a deepening consciousness of the existence of two kinds of power in the disintegrating society that had once been the Tsardom. There was the Provisional Government ("Provisional" was a title that spoke volumes), mainly made up of those who had been deputies in the dissolved Duma: these enjoyed assent, if not allegiance, from the chiefs of a civil service which was sagging and from military chiefs of an army which was already beginning to crumble. But there was also this newly elected "Soviet" in Petrograd, this utterly unexpected birth of revolution, something with power the extent of which had yet to be gauged.

Nevertheless the hope was reposed in this temporary Government, headed by Prince Lvov, that under its guidance Russia would be regenerated and that the proof of this would soon be seen in a vigorous mustering of anti-German forces. This hope immediately shines through the concluding words of the glowing editorial of the *Manchester Guardian*, then the 'undisputed sovereign' of the European Liberal press:

"The Revolution in Russia is the deadliest blow to the war morale of Germany that has been struck. That it will strengthen Russia in the further conduct of the war as well as liberalise the spirit and purpose for which she wages war – these are certainties. It is the reactionaries who have now been struck down who worked for a separate peace and an alliance with Germany. They were kindred souls with the Junkers. They feared liberty in Russia much more than the German enemy, and to stave off free institutions they were prepared to lop off provinces.

"It is the Liberals of Russia who have resisted these unholy temptations, and now that they have taken over the control we may hope that a new vigour will energise the war, springing from a sincere idealism. Revolution has before now proved a great mother of efficiency, and there is no finer dynamic force than a passion for freedom. England hails the new Russia with a higher hope and a surer confidence in the future not only of this war but of the world." *(16.iii.1917)*

The composition of the Provisional Government seemed likely to embody the aspirations not only of advanced Liberalism but also of Right-wing Conservatism, with its war-aim of 'a knock-out blow'; for the *Morning Post* of March 17, giving the list[7] of the new Russian cabinet, headlined it "The new Cabinet: a pro-Entente body."

7 The Soviets

The other centre of power was this new phenomenon, called a Soviet, or Council of Workers' and Soldiers' Deputies, which had appeared on the morrow of the armed rising in Petrograd. What was this body? A similar body had come into existence at the end of the year 1905 during the unsuccessful 1905-07 Revolution. It had now sprung up again in the main towns of European Russia, and then, as the news spread, in towns of other parts of the far-flung Russian Empire. It was true that in a peculiarly slipshod way the Petrograd Soviet, almost in the course of its coming together and assembling (being as it were unconscious of its own power) had handed over nearly everything in the way of authority to the government that its leaders insisted should be formed from a few members of the extremely unrepresentative Duma.

Where the drive came from was disclosed in the *Manchester Guardian*, which at this time and for at least a twelve-month afterwards had a clearer notion of what was happening than other British daily papers. "The initiative in the revolutionary movement", it wrote on Friday March 16, "came from the working classes …. It was at a later stage that the Duma came in." On the next day, Saturday March 17, the editorial dealing with "the nature of the elements ranged on the side of freedom", explained first that "roughly" there were two wings – the Left and the Moderates, each with their own organisation.

"It is the Left who made the Revolution and have given direction to the whole movement at every critical stage. They organised the workmen for the general strike, and they organised the soldiers to take the side of the workmen when the outbreak came."

The Left, who "control the working men and the troops", had participated on Tuesday March 13 in a debate in the *right* wing of the Taurida Palace and "it persuaded the Duma" to constitute the Provisional Government. The Duma committee (mainly Monarchists) had got no further that morning than to implore the Tsar by telegram to appoint a new responsible cabinet.

Apart from the strange lumping together in "the Left" of the Bolshevik Party, whose leaders were mostly in Siberian exile or abroad, with the other socialist parties whose leaders carried through this deal with the Duma, the willingness of the elected Committee of the Soviet, meeting in the left wing of the Taurida Palace, to build up and support the Provisional Government was made clear enough in the *Manchester Guardian*. It was a comforting thought for many in Britain that maybe the Soviet supporting and "supervising" the new Government was not so fundamentally different from the British Labour's support of Lloyd George's new coalition Cabinet in Britain.

But there remained in those early days the disturbing thought that the soldiers seemed to be taking orders from the Soviet; and that the Petrograd Soviet had assumed the right to issue such orders, the outstanding and indeed upsetting example being *Prikaz* (or Order) No 1. Dated March 14, it ordered that committees were to be elected in all military and naval units to exercise control of all use of weapons within the Petrograd Military District; that civilian rights were to be given to soldiers and sailors; and that the privileges of the officers were to be abolished. In their political action, units were to be subject to these committees and to the Petrograd Soviet. Orders from any other source were to be obeyed only if not contradicting those of the Soviet. Furthermore, arms were to be under the control of the committees and were not to be surrendered if officers demanded it. On duty, strict discipline was to be preserved but salutes off duty were abolished and usages as between officer and ratings in the navy or non-commissioned ranks in the army were to be in democratic form. This order was presently to be reinforced by the stipulation that in the armed forces the death penalty was abolished.

This far-reaching order aroused further questionings as to what would happen with the Soviet. Would it continue to support the Provisional Government? Was it to be a loyal opposition, in all main questions supporting the Government while retaining the right of criticism? Was not its freedom, particularly for its 'extremists', about to border on licence? Could it be made to run in harness with the Government so as to become a really useful body for the successful prosecution of the war?

Furthermore, was it the right sort of body? Should there not have been delegates from unions?[8] Delegates from existing societies and working-class organisations?

Was it not something which had grown up in the moment of revolution and as an organ that could reflect the changes in the view and feelings of the soldiers in the barracks and regiments and of the workers in the factory and the sailors in the fleet? Could this possibly be a stable or a useful body? Was it not altogether too democratic?

Such were the questionings in Britain, questionings loaded by the outlook of the various strata of English society.

All these questions were mounting up in the minds of those who read the rapidly shifting and changing news of the Revolution. Altogether it may be said in that month of April 1917 the question was being asked: What sort of revolution is it in Russia?

Curiously enough, essentially the same questions were being asked inside the borders of Russia. The parties in the Provisional Government whose business it was to carry through the democratic revolution gave varying answers. It was at this point that Lenin arrived. His arrival on April 16 at the Finland Station, and his arguments then and during the next few weeks, put an entirely new complexion upon affairs. He had to argue for days against other leading members of the Bolshevik Party openly in the columns of *Pravda*. He had to argue inside Party meetings. He had to argue inside meetings of the Soviet; and finally, when he had won over the Bolshevik Party to his standpoint, he had to put forward argument after argument in the various congresses that were beginning to meet, Congresses of Peasants, Congresses of Soviets and all kinds of other sudden expressions of the newly born democracy.

8 The nature of a revolution

What kind of revolution was it? If diagnosed as one or another species of the genus revolution, then forecasts could be made of its probable course. What kind, what species? In 1917 the answer to this question from outside Russia was being variously given in different countries. In a few countries of Asia it might appear simply as an overthrow of a despotism, of an autocratic government. In the course of the innumerable revolutions of European and of Asiatic history such an overthrow invariably had been succeeded, after turmoil, by a new stage when either another member of the same dynasty had been chosen as ruler or a new dynasty, equally autocratic, had been imposed with an entirely new emperor. This, in the main, had been the history of civilised mankind from China to Peru, from the empires of antiquity to one European monarchy after another.

There were, however, very few in 20th century Britain who could hold that standpoint. To explain what kind of revolution it was, the Fleet Street newspapers with their retinue of part-time writers from the universities had recourse to historic parallels. On the one hand the *Morning Post* assumed that it was like "the Glorious Revolution" of 1688, sometimes called the Whig Revolution, by which King James II was deposed and his Dutch son-in-law, William of Orange, was crowned by grace of the great ruling families of England – or as Bertrand Russell, great-grandson of the sixth Duke of Bedford, was to put it:

> "My family stood for liberty, suffered for it; for this cause we got rid of James II and hired another king."

Some, however, thought that there was a parallel with the Great Rebellion against the despotic rule of King Charles I which was to result eventually in a government responsible to Parliament. This they expected, and hoped, would hatch out of the egg in Russia. For others, who had moved forward a century or so, the explanation was to be found in a parallel with the great French Revolution that shook feudal Europe at the end of the 18th century; and Russia at the beginning of the 20th century was still a semi-feudal society.

To socialists, especially on the continent of Europe, there was no mystery about it, no dubiety. The leaders of these big Social-Democratic parties with their extensive daily newspaper press and corps of writers in numerous other periodicals were all practitioners of a social science the groundwork of which they derived from the economic and historical doctrines of Karl Marx. For them the only revolutions worthy of study were social revolutions, in which one mode of production gave way to another and a new class strode on to the stage of history and took the leading role. In modern times this meant the supersession of the feudal system by the capitalist or bourgeois mode of production and the coming supersession of the latter by the socialist mode of production – or, in terms sanctioned by long usage, the bourgeois-democratic revolution to be followed, after an interval which might be long or short, by the proletarian-socialist revolution. So much was clearly indicated by the experience of Europe over nearly four centuries.

In the 20th century in every country where the new capitalist mode of production had come to prevail, with it developed the working class. In Russia there were still the peasants in their overwhelming numbers, as in the rest of Europe, with the exception of England where in the 18th century the peasantry had been liquidated as a class. If these two classes, one new, the working class, and one a survival from earlier times, the peasantry, were now both driving forces in the bourgeois-democratic revolution then entirely new questions came up for settlement. Which class was to lead?

Then further, since objectively in most countries of Europe conditions were mature for the transition to socialism, how long need the interval be between the bourgeois-democratic and the proletarian-socialist revolution? Or could the one grow over immediately into the other? On these questions there was no unanimity among socialists. Yet on the answer to these questions, depending on a correct analysis of the situation and the class forces, would hang the strategy and tactics of the classes and parties involved.

But most important of all was the fact that a revolution was taking place in the midst of a European war, and at a moment when it was becoming a world war with the entry of China, North America and South America. The impact of the Russian Revolution on contemporary socialist thinking in Europe and in Britain was particularly conditioned by this last circumstance. The overwhelming majority of the Labour movement in Britain through their various means of expression had solidly supported the war of the Entente against the central empires. For them the Russian Revolution, and any judgment of it, was inseparable from the overriding needs of 'national defence' against the German menace.

This too was the standpoint as we have seen of those socialist parties or sections of parties who had obtained the majority in the Petrograd Soviet and then in the Congress of Soviets.

In Britain, both for rulers and ruled – and for socialists other than a small minority – the question of the war conditioned the impact of the Russian Revolution.

For those who in Russia had to solve the question of the kind of revolution it was, the policy to be followed was also conditioned by the connection of the Revolution and the war. They were not only inseparable: but, as will be seen, in many writings both before the war and during it, it was Lenin's view that the war itself was caused by capitalism in its 20th century development. Monopoly capitalism, imperialism, was the cause of war, he had argued. To end the war it was necessary to end imperialism. To overthrow the government of the warmongers was a slogan which could only mean the overthrow of capitalism. There could be no question at all of a working-class body which remained true to international socialism participating in the 'defence of their country', even under the mask of 'revolutionary defence'. So when Lenin arrived at the Finland Station in Petrograd on April 16, 1917, he was ready with the answer to the question – what kind of revolution is it, and what are its prospects? That night he elaborated the famous *April Theses*.[9] It is clear that a complete negation of the war was also the negation of the capitalist government that was responsible for the war and for pursuing it.

9   Lenin's *April Theses*

Lenin's *April Theses*, written on the morrow of his arrival on April 17, 1917, and submitted that same day to meetings of Bolsheviks, Mensheviks and some others was and, indeed, is an extraordinary document. Historians may regard it as more important than the theses nailed by Martin Luther to the door of the church at Wittenberg. They indicated something new which startled many of his own comrades, upset Mensheviks and Socialist-Revolutionaries, and frightened parties of the bourgeoisie. The *April Theses* were a scientifically based plan of struggle for the transition from the bourgeois-democratic to the socialist revolution. First and foremost they defined "our attitude" to the war, the most vital of all the issues then facing the peoples of Russia and of the world. The war, said Lenin, was still a predatory and imperialist war owing to the capitalist nature of the new government of Lvov and Co, which could not wage any other kind of war but an imperialist war. It was *impossible* to end the war by a truly democratic peace without the overthrow of capitalism. He called for no annexations, and widespread explanations to the troops.

His second thesis showed that the specific feature of the February Revolution was that it represented a *transition* from the first stage of the Revolution – "which, owing to the insufficient class consciousness and organisation of the proletariat, placed power in the hands of the bourgeoisie" – to the second stage which must place power "in the hands of the proletariat and the poorest sections of the peasants". Hence, in Thesis No 3, "no support for the Provisional Government"; and, in No 4, that "our Party" being in a small minority so far in most Soviets, must "present a patient, systematic and persistent explanation" of errors and at the same time "we preach the necessity of transferring the entire state power to the Soviets of Workers' Deputies", so that the people may by experience overcome their mistakes. Thesis No 5 may be quoted in full.

"Not a parliamentary republic – to return to a parliamentary republic from the Soviets of Workers' Deputies would be a retrograde step – but a republic of Soviets of Workers', Agricultural Labourers' and Peasants' Deputies throughout the country, from top to bottom.
"Abolition of the police, the army and the bureaucracy.[10]
"The salaries of all officials, all of whom are elective and displaceable at any time, not to exceed the average wage of a competent worker."

Thesis No 6, the agrarian programme, which was to emphasise the Soviets of Agricultural Labourers' Deputies, included "confiscation of all landed estates"; while, in No 7, all banks were to be amalgamated into a single bank which should be supervised by the Soviet. No 8 stated:

"It is not our *immediate* task to 'introduce' socialism, but only to bring social production and the distribution of products at once under the *control* of the Soviets of Workers' Deputies."

An immediate summons to a Party congress and alterations to the Party programme were included in No 9, and thirdly "(c) A new name for the Party."[11]

The coping stone was put on these proposals with the 10th Thesis, namely:

"A new International.
"We must take the initiative in creating a revolutionary International, an International against the *social-chauvinists* and against the 'Centre'[12]."

His hearers were both astonished and appalled. The *Theses* ran counter to what they had in their minds. They revealed the serious confusion which had been shared by leaders such as Kamenev, Stalin and Muranov, just back from exile in Siberia –

but not by young Molotov then, at the age of 26, playing a prominent part in Petrograd.

There was fierce controversy until, as Lenin later explained:

"Both the theses and my report gave rise to differences of opinion amongst the Bolsheviks themselves and the editors of *Pravda*. After a number of consultations we unanimously concluded that it would be advisable openly to discuss our differences and thus provide material for the All-Russia Conference of our Party".[13]

So the *Theses* were printed on April 26. In the discussion in the press, Kamenev attacked Lenin's theses and said the Party ought not to aim at the transition to a socialist revolution but to the completion of the bourgeois-democratic revolution. In articles and pamphlets Lenin stressed the creative nature of Marxist theory and the danger of dogmatism:

"It is essential to grasp the incontestable truth that a Marxist must take cognisance of real life, of the true facts of *reality*, and not cling to a theory of yesterday, which, like all theories, at best only outlines the main and general, only *comes near* to embracing life in all its complexities. 'Theory, my friend, is grey, but green is the eternal tree of life.'"[14]

He went on to say:

"To deal with the question of 'completion' of the bourgeois revolution in the old way is to sacrifice living Marxism to the dead letter.
"According to the old way of thinking, the rule of the bourgeoisie could and should be followed by the rule of the proletariat and the peasantry, by their dictatorship.
"In real life, however, things have *already* turned out *differently*; there has been an extremely original, novel and unprecedented *interlacing of the one with the other*. We have side by side, existing together, simultaneously, *both* the rule of the bourgeoisie (the government of Lvov and Guchkov) and a revolutionary-democratic dictatorship of the proletariat and the peasantry, which is voluntarily ceding power to the bourgeoisie, *voluntarily* making itself an appendage of the bourgeoisie."[15]

But, if some of the Bolshevik leaders were hard to convince, it can be imagined the effect the theses had on the others who listened to them on April 17, at a meeting at the Taurida Palace where the Soviet held its sessions. Bogdanov interrupted with cries of "Delirium, the delirium of a madman". Steklov, editor of *Izvestia*, said Lenin's speech consisted of "abstract constructions" which he would abandon when he got to know the Russian situation. George Plekhanov, once the acknowledged leading theorist of the Russian Social-Democratic Labour Party, in an article in his newspaper *Yedinstvo (Unity)* wrote of Lenin's speech as "the speech of a madman". He quoted the words of the Menshevik Chkheidze, saying "Lenin alone will remain outside the revolutions, and we shall go our own way."

A campaign of slander was launched against Lenin: lies and inventions of the lowest kind were put about in the bourgeois press, primarily directed against Lenin. It was suggested that he was "pro-German". This attack, which developed especially after the Party Conference in May, did not cease thereafter. In some parts of the world, in some nooks and crannies of counter-revolution, there are people today who still believe some of these wild lies and inventions that were manufactured to blacken the name of Lenin and to prevent his influence spreading rapidly amongst the workers.

The discussion went on for days and then for weeks. But the clarity and penetrating power of Lenin's arguments defeated the rhetoric of his opponents. It is recorded in the report of the 7th Party Conference that, at the Petrograd City Conference beginning on April 27, one delegate had said: "Before Lenin arrived all the comrades were wandering in the dark." It was two weeks after the Revolution that Kamenev and Stalin and others reached Petrograd. It was five weeks before Lenin arrived to put them straight. When the Petrograd City Conference was held on April 27 it had the effect of a rehearsal for the 7th All-Russia Conference of the Russian Social-Democratic Labour Party.

On May 1 Milyukov, Minister of Foreign Affairs, was responsible for a Note to the Allies stating that "the whole people desire to continue the world war until a decisive victory is achieved, and that the Provisional Government intends fully to observe the obligations undertaken towards our Allies". Milyukov's Note was published on May 2. In Petrograd on May 3 and 4 vast crowds of workers and soldiers marched in demonstrations to the seat of the Provisional Government, demonstrating against Milyukov's Note and carrying banners with the demands "Publish the Secret Treaties!", "Down with the War!", "All power to the Soviets!" This was within a fortnight from the writing of the *April Theses*.

On May 15 a new Provisional Government was formed. The first government had lasted only two months from the mid-March to the mid-May; the first coalition government was now formed. It included two Mensheviks, and two SRs, one of them Kerensky, who now became Minster for War.

In the midst of this critical situation the 7th Conference of the Russian Social-Democratic Labour Party (Bolsheviks) met from May 7 until May 12. It was the first time that a Bolshevik Conference had met openly. It showed the very rapid growth of the Party. What in mid-March had been some 24,000 had already become 80,000.

Lenin reported on the task of the Party. This, he said, was to effect the transition from the first stage which had placed power in the hands of the bourgeoisie "to the second stage which must place power in the hands of the proletariat and the poorest strata of the peasantry".[16] The Party should prepare for the Socialist Revolution and the slogan was "All power to the Soviets". This meant that the dual power must come to an end, landlords and capitalists must be driven out of the government and that the Soviets should become the sovereign power in Russia. By the end of the Conference Bolshevik leaders who had opposed Lenin from April 27 up till then were now forced to accept his standpoint. In a general discussion on the national question those who were opposed to the right of nations of self-determination were also defeated. Not only in the Petrograd City Conference of April 27 up to May 5, but in a whole series of local conferences and factory conferences, the Bolshevik workers in the factories had shown themselves, by overwhelming majorities, in favour of the standpoint taken up by V I Lenin in his ten theses.

There was that spring and early summer no country in the world so free as Russia. Conference after conference went on throughout the summer. A Petrograd Conference of Factory Committees was held from June 12 to 16 and a majority, nearly 3 to 1, supported the Bolsheviks. This majority was to grow throughout the summer. On June 16 there met the first All-Russian Congress of Soviets of Workers', Soldiers' and Peasants' Deputies. There were 822 delegates with voting rights. Of these, the Bolsheviks were still very much in the minority; there were 285 SRs, 248 Mensheviks and 105 Bolsheviks, while 150 belonged to various minor groups and 45 had no party allegiance at all. This was an indication of the still confused and fluid outlook of the mass of representatives of the people in the new democracy.

Notes and References

1   Together with the press of Fleet Street there was one paper from the rest of Great Britain which was ranked with the Fleet Street press partly because it also had a national circulation. This was the *Manchester Guardian*, edited by C P Scott throughout half a century.

2   Actually this had first been published in Spring 1912, only to fold up into a weekly in the Autumn of 1914. Its more official rival the *Daily Citizen* had appeared in the Autumn of 1912 and survived until early Summer of 1915 when it folded up entirely.

3   See Section 5, 'Impact on the Labour Movement'.

4   For example, issue No 44 of February 8 contains two half columns beginning as follows:
"In Russia. *The Social Democrat*, a Russian Socialist paper published by Lenin's group in Geneva, Switzerland, (December 30, 1916) gives the text of a leaflet published in October by the Petrograd Committee of the Social-Democratic Labour Party of Russia."
The ignorance of parties and events in Russia so widespread in Fleet Street was not shared by *The Call*, as may be seen by harking back ten weeks to the beginning of the year 1917, when its 39th issue on January 4 contained an article by John Bryan ('International Socialism is now a heap of ruin, a mass of treachery, an accumulation of faithless cynicism and demoralisation') and another headed 'Russian Socialists and the International' by G Chicherine.

5   Arthur Henderson MP, Labour War Cabinet, Honorary President Iron Founders' Trade Union; John Hodge MP, Minister of Labour, General Secretary, British Steelsmelters' Trade Union; George N Barnes MP, Minister of Pensions (Amalgamated Society of Engineers); William Brace MP, Under Secretary to the Home

Office (South Wales Miners' Federation); Stephen Walsh MP, Parliamentary Secretary to National Service Department (Lancashire and Cheshire Miners' Federation); George H Roberts MP, Parliamentary Secretary to Board of Trade (Typographical Trade Union); James Parker MP, Chief Whip Labour Party; George J Wardle MP, Chairman Parliamentary Labour Party; Charles Duncan MP, Secretary Parliamentary Labour Party; John Hill JP, Chairman Parliamentary Committee Trades Union Congress; C W Bowerman MP, Secretary Parliamentary Committee Trades Union Congress; Frank Purdy, Chairman Labour Party National Executive; James O'Grady MP, Chairman General Federation of Trades Unions; W A Appleton, Secretary General Federation of Trades Unions; Harry Gosling JP, President Transport Workers Federation; James Sexton JP, Vice-President Transport Workers' Federation; J T Bromlie, Chairman Amalgamated Society of Engineers; Will Thorne MP, General Secretary Gas Workers' and General Labourers' Trade Union; Alexander Wilkie MP, Secretary Ship Constructors' and Shipwrights' Association; and J H Thomas MP, Secretary National Union of Railwaymen.

6   The shop steward William Gallacher, travelling on business of the Clyde Workers Committee to London, noticed the bill, 'The Blatant Beast' by Blatchford and assumed it referred to the Kaiser. On purchasing the journal he found it referred to himself.

7   Premier, Minister of the Interior and President of the Council: Prince Lvov, President of the Alliance of Zemstvos.
Minister for Foreign Affairs: P Milyukov, Deputy for Petrograd.
Minister of Justice: A Kerensky, Deputy for Saratov.
Minister of Ways and Communications: N Nekrasov, Vice-President of the Duma.
Minister of Commerce and Industry: A Konovalov, Deputy for Kostroma.
Minister of Public Instruction: Professor A Manuilov, of Moscow University.
Minister of War and Marine, *ad interim:* A Guchkov, member of the Council of the Empire, former President of the third Duma and President of the United Committees of Mobilised Industry.
Minister of Agriculture: A Schingarev, Deputy for Petrograd.
Minister of Finance: M Tereshchenko, Deputy for Kiev.
Controller of State: M Godunev, Deputy for Kazan.
(*Reuters*, Petrograd, 15 March 1917)

8   Under Tsarism trade unions in so far as they were permitted legally had a much circumscribed existence.

9   See Section 9 and Appendix.

10 *ie*, the standing army to be replaced by the arming of the whole people.

11 Lenin's footnote: "Instead of 'Social-Democracy', whose official leaders throughout the world have betrayed socialism and deserted to the bourgeoisie (the 'defencists' and the vacillating 'Kautskyites'), we must call ourselves the Communist Party."

12 Lenin's footnote: "The 'Centre' in the international Social-Democratic movement is the trend which vacillates between the chauvinists (= 'defencists') and internationalists, *ie* Kautsky and Co in Germany, Longuet and Co in France, Chkheidze and Co in Russia, Turati and Co in Italy, MacDonald and Co in Britain etc."

13 Lenin, 'Foreword' to *Letters on Tactics*, in *Collected Works*, Vol 24, p 42 –Ed.

14 Lenin, first *Letter on Tactics*, in *ibid*, p 45 (RPA mistakenly attributes the quotation to Lenin's article *The Dual Power – Ed*).

15 *Ibid*, pp 45-6.

16 This quotation appears to come from the *April Theses*, rather from Lenin's reported speeches to the Conference –*Ed*.

Appendix

The *April Theses*

Submitted by V I Lenin, April 17, 1917[1]

1) In our attitude towards the war, which under the new government of Lvov and Co unquestionably remains on Russia's part a predatory imperialist war owing to the capitalist nature of that government, not the slightest concession to 'revolutionary defencism' is permissible.

The class-conscious proletariat can give its consent to a revolutionary war, which would really justify revolutionary defencism, only on condition: (a) that the power pass to the proletariat and the poorest sections of the peasants aligned with the proletariat; (b) that all annexations be renounced in deed and not in word; (c) that a complete break be effected in actual fact with all capitalist interests.

In view of the undoubted honesty of those broad sections of the mass believers in revolutionary defencism who accept the war only as a necessity, and not as a means of conquest, in view of the fact that they are being deceived by the bourgeoisie, it is necessary with particular thoroughness, persistence and patience to explain their error to them, to explain the inseparable connection existing between capital and the imperialist war, and to prove that without overthrowing capital *it is impossible* to end the war by a truly democratic peace, a peace not imposed by violence.

The most widespread campaign for this view must be organised in the army at the front.

Fraternisation.

2) The specific feature of the present situation in Russia is that the country is *passing* from the first stage of the revolution – which, owing to the insufficient class consciousness and organisation of the proletariat, placed power in the hands of the bourgeoisie – to its *second* stage, which must place power in the hands of the proletariat and the poorest sections of the peasants.

This transition is characterised, on the one hand, by a maximum of legally recognised rights (Russia is now the freest of all the belligerent countries in the world); on the other, by the absence of violence towards the masses, and, finally, by their unreasoning trust in the government of capitalists, those worst enemies of peace and socialism.

This peculiar situation demands of us an ability to adapt ourselves to the special conditions of Party work among unprecedentedly large masses of proletarians who have just awakened to political life.

3) No support for the Provisional Government; the utter falsity of all its

promises should be made clear, particularly of those relating to the renunciation of annexations. Exposure in place of the impermissible, illusion-breeding 'demand' that *this* government, a government of capitalists, should cease to be an imperialist government.

4) Recognition of the fact that in most of the Soviets of Workers' Deputies our Party is in a minority, so far a small minority, as against a *bloc of all* the petty-bourgeois opportunist elements, from the Popular Socialists and the Socialist-Revolutionaries down to the Organising Committee (Chkheidze, Tsereteli etc), Steklov etc etc, who have yielded to the influence of the bourgeoisie and spread that influence among the proletariat.

The masses must be made to see that the Soviets of Workers' Deputies are *the only possible* form of revolutionary government, and that therefore our task is, as long as *this* government yields to the influence of the bourgeoisie, to present a patient, systematic, and persistent explanation of the errors of their tactics, an explanation especially adapted to the practical needs of the masses.

As long as we are in the minority we carry on the work of criticising and exposing errors and at the same time we preach the necessity of transferring the entire state power to the Soviets of Workers' Deputies, so that the people may overcome their mistakes by experience.

5) Not a parliamentary republic – to return to a parliamentary republic from the Soviets of Workers' Deputies would be a retrograde step – but a republic of Soviets of Workers', Agricultural Labourers' and Peasants' Deputies throughout the country, from top to bottom.

Abolition of the police, the army and the bureaucracy.

The salaries of all officials, all of whom are elective and displaceable at any time, not to exceed the average wage of a competent worker.

6) The weight of emphasis in the agrarian programme to be shifted to the Soviets of Agricultural Labourers' Deputies.

Confiscation of all landed estates.

Nationalisation of *all* lands in the country, the land to be disposed of by the local Soviets of Agricultural Labourers' and Peasants' Deputies. The organisation of separate Soviets of Deputies of Poor Peasants. The setting up of a model farm on each of the large estates (ranging in size from 100 to 300 dessiatines, according to local and other conditions, and to the decisions of the local bodies) under the control of the Soviets of Agricultural Labourers' Deputies and for the public account.

7) The immediate amalgamation of all banks in the country into a single national bank, and the institution of control over it by the Soviet of Workers' Deputies.

8) It is not our *immediate* task to 'introduce' socialism, but only to bring social production and the distribution of products at once under the *control* of the Soviets

of Workers' Deputies.

9) Party tasks:

(a) Immediate convocation of a Party congress;

(b) Alteration of the Party Programme, mainly:

(1) On the question of imperialism and the imperialist war,

(2) On our attitude towards the state and our demand for a "commune state"[2];

(3) Amendment of our out-of-date minimum programme;

(c) Change of the Party's name.

10) A new International.

We must take the initiative in creating a revolutionary International, an International against the *social-chauvinists* and against the 'Centre'.

Notes

1   Here, and in the extracts in Ch 1, the translation is taken from Lenin, *Collected Works*, Vol 24, Progress, Moscow, 1964, pp 21-24, rather than that given originally by RPA –*Ed*.

2   *ie*, a state of which the Paris Commune was the prototype.

2 Empire and War

1 Who meets what?

The impact of the Russian Revolution throughout the whole world was immense but diversified. There was nothing uniform in its effect, which differed from country to country, and within each country. Furthermore the Revolution itself changed and developed, and with these changes the impact on peoples and classes altered.

To gauge the impact of the Russian Revolution on Britain throughout the year 1917 and after, a brief glance must first of all be cast upon the historic relations between the two countries.

It was the prospect of trade that drew together England and Russia from opposite ends of Europe and linked the Tudor monarchy with the rulers of Muscovy. When the Emperor of Russia, Ivan the Terrible, wrote to Queen Elizabeth, treaties and embassies followed, while the visit to the court in London of "Russian grandees, dropping pearls and vermin" recall some jocular lines in the plays of Shakespeare.[1] In *A Brief History of Moscovia* Milton surveyed a half century of Anglo-Russian relations, from 1553 to 1604, condemned the absolute power of the Tsar, and compassionately wrote that "there are no people that live so miserably as the poor of Russia". Trade grew, and with it a growing interest in Russia is reflected in English literature. Contacts became closer, from the late 17th century when the young Romanov Tsar, Peter the Great, came to London and wrought at his shipwright's task in Deptford, to the days when William Pitt was the valued friend of Vorontsov, Ambassador to the Court of St James from the Empress Catherine II, that Empress of whom Byron was to write:

"In Catherine's reign, whom glory still adores
 As greatest of all sovereigns and w ... s."

On the Russian side similarly, relations developed, with the great poet Pushkin drawing on the wells of English literature; and after him the line of giants that were to put Russian writing in the front rank of world literature. Shakespeare, Scott and Byron appeared in Russian dress; Tolstoy, Turgenev and Chekhov in English; and this mutuality in art and literature became a tradition that can be seen today in Marshak's lapidary version of Robert Burns. Russian music, Russian ballet and other kinds of art became acclimatised in Britain. In all these centuries Britain and Russia had often been at war with major powers of Europe, but never with each other – except on the single occasion of the Crimean War. Otherwise the two states had centuries of friendly relations, which had begun with the very beginnings of capitalist society in Britain, on the basis of East-West trade.

When after the battle of Waterloo in 1815 the monarchs of Europe had reseated the Bourbon King Louis XVlll upon the throne of France, they fondly hoped they had finally extinguished the last embers of the French Revolution. There were a dozen or more monarchies in Europe but Russia and Britain were outstanding. The one had the greatest space and the greatest population in Europe, the other had command of the seas. Indeed, the maritime power of Britain expanded until it had almost a near monopoly of the world market, while the British navy was to be supreme from Trafalgar onwards for a hundred years without a rival. Between the two great powers at either end of Europe there were continuing similarities but also growing differences. Externally there was an immense concentration of power in each. Internally the differences could be seen.

In their social systems Russia and Britain diverged more and more as the years went on. The United Kingdom was the oldest country of capitalism and also the most developed. Within twenty years after Waterloo it was to see the manufacturers, the new capitalist class, the owners of mines and mills, taking over positions previously the preserve of the landed gentry and the merchant princes. The 'millocracy' was beginning to oust the aristocracy from the seats of power. It was the triumph of the bourgeoisie over the old oligarchy. By the mid-century Britain had become the "most bourgeois of all nations", aiming, as Engels said in 1858, to possess "a bourgeois aristocracy and a bourgeois proletariat, as well as a bourgeoisie".[2] Britain became for a while the mart of universal trade and the workshop of the world. It was the capitalist country par excellence.

Russia on the other hand had remained predominantly a feudal country. Its output was overwhelmingly agricultural, produced by serfs on vast estates where, in some cases, scores of thousands of serfs were owned by a single family. Their serfdom, though disturbed by the recurrent risings of the peasants, was not abolished till 1861. It was only after this emancipation of the serfs that there could be effective capitalist development in Russia. But right up to the end of the next half-century, Russia remained a land of huge estates on which the peasants remained socially, economically and politically at the mercy of the landowners, with an archipelago of towns amid a sea of peasantry and peasant villages. Capitalism was developing and with it the capitalist class and also a new working class; but the government remained as it had been in past centuries, a military bureaucracy headed by an autocrat who represented the interests of the landlord class and was himself the supreme landlord in all the Russias.

2 The clash of empires

Beneath these friendly relations there was, in Victorian times, a growing tension and edginess. This was due not so much to their differences – the growing contrast between the development of liberal institutions in the one country and the insistence in the other on the maintenance in its full rigour of autocracy – as to their similarities.

Each was a hereditary monarchy. Each possessed orders of nobility. Each was composed of a central area – Great Britain and Great Russia – surrounded by subordinate states, dependencies, colonies, nations, tribes, protectorates and spheres of influence. In each empire the outlying parts were put under viceroys (Ireland, Canada, India) or governors-general; and these outlying parts were also used for political prisoners who were sentenced to transportation either to Botany Bay until a century ago, or to Siberia – which latter was in use right up to 1917.

In the vast continent of Asia, round the edges of the two empires, friction could easily develop, for real or imaginary causes. There was friction over the Ottoman Empire of the Turks, especially over what was called Turkey-in-Europe which then comprised most of the Balkans as well as Constantinople and the Straits. The Crimean War in the 1850s had been fought on what was to happen to this "sick man of Europe", as Tsar Nicholas I phrased it. Twenty years later there was nearly another war with the warmongers singing a chorus that created the word "jingoism", namely:

"We don't want to fight, but, by jingo if we do,
We've got the ships, we've got the men, we've got the money too.
We've fought the Bear before, and while Britons shall be true,
The Russians shall not have Constantinople."

The first effective anti-war movement in Britain, and also the first counter-agitation to jingoism, was led in 1877 by the poet William Morris, afterwards a pioneer of socialism in Britain. The threat of war receded. But eight years later, when the Russians had established a railhead at Pendjeh near the Afghan border and beside the ruins of old Merv, it induced in British ruling circles and in their troupe of attendant journalists an attack of jitters, afterwards dubbed 'Mervousness'. Another few years, and this time Persia seemed at stake. Then, at the century's end, rivalry developed in China between the British sphere of influence in the torrid zone and 'the Russian Bear prowling down from the frozen North'. China had become 'the sick man of Asia', and the rival vultures were hovering over his body. It was imagined, in defiance of logistics, that the proximity of Russia-in-Asia, across impassable mountains and deserts, constituted a danger to British supremacy in India.[3]

These Asiatic apprehensions, which were to recur in a new form after 1917, were stilled in the 20th century by the emergence of a deeper and sharper antagonism between militarist Germany and navalist Britain. For it was not only Russia and Britain that had developed differently. There was uneven development generally in a Europe where the capitalist mode of production had come to prevail in one industry after another. In particular, after the Franco-Prussian War of 1870-71, the new German Empire had rapidly begun to overtake Britain in home production and to become its chief commercial competitor. In the 20th century this became the rivalry of imperialist powers.

At the beginning of the century an atlas of the London School Board listed in order of size the principal empires of the world. The list began with the British Empire, covering an area of well nigh 12m square miles. The Russian Empire came next with over 8m; France and her colonies had 4⅓m; United States and her colonies 3¾m square miles. Then came Germany and her colonies with a little over 1m square miles, the Turkish Empire with 1½m square miles and then a number of lesser empires, the lot amounting to perhaps a dozen out of the 60 to 70 sovereign states of the world. Most of the land surface of the continent of Africa was made up of colonies. The growing rivalry between empires was due to the fact that all the colonial countries had been divided up by the first decade of the twentieth century. Further expansion would only be reached by redivision.

As far back as the first year of the century Britain was seeking for understandings or alliances. These were often expressed in treaties or agreements, couched in general terms. But associated with the formal documents there were secret clauses, military and political, never to be disclosed to the unsuspecting public, which would find themselves plunged in war, or upon the brink, and never knew the real causes. Already there was in Europe the Triple Alliance between the German Empire, the Austro-Hungarian Empire and the Kingdom of Italy. There was also the Franco-Russian Alliance which had been built up for over a dozen years. Following on the Anglo-Japanese military and naval alliance in 1902, an understanding was sought with France. This, in the agreements of April 8, 1904, took the shape of an Entente Cordiale or cordial understanding, a deal between the British and French Empires. So concessions were made over the Newfoundland fisheries and over frontiers where the two Empires had clashed in Equatorial Africa. But it was over two North African countries that this understanding was reached. In Article I, while His Britannic Majesty's Government declared that they had no intention of altering the political status of Egypt which they had occupied since 1823, the French Government declared "that they will not obstruct the action of Great Britain in that country by asking that a limit of time be fixed for the British occupation or in any other manner". Similarly, on the question of Morocco, the French Government declared they had no intention of altering its political status, whereupon His Majesty's Government recognised that it appertained to France to preserve order in Morocco and to provide assistance for the purpose of all administrative, economic, financial and military reforms which it may require; where His Majesty's Government declared *they* would not obstruct the action taken by France for this purpose. There were 5 secret articles in the agreements. Finally it was declared that neither would annex more territory in South-East Asia, but that Siam (now Thailand) would be divided into British and French spheres of influence, the British sphere being west of the Menam Basin and the French sphere east of it. Such was the Entente

Cordiale, which was to be a model of how these understandings between the empires, ostensibly in order to keep the peace and to diminish causes of friction, were made at the beginning of this century.

3   The Anglo-Russian Entente

The French model was followed in the endeavour to reach an understanding between Britain and Russia by removal of the causes of friction, mainly as before at the expense of other countries. The first stage was reached in the midst of the 1905-07 Revolution. A loan of £11m, by permission of the Foreign Office, was raised in 1906 on the London Stock Exchange, which thus threw in its resources as a backing to the millions of francs (to the value some £80m) which French investors had put into Russian bonds. The effect was to bolster up the regime of Tsardom which throughout 1905 had been suffering heavy blows after defeat in the 1904-05 war with Japan, the metropolitan strikes suppressed by the massacre of Bloody Sunday on January 22, 1905, the mutiny of the battleship *Potemkin* in June 1905 and finally the series of general strikes in Russian cities. The Tsar had been compelled to grant a sort of Parliament. This had met in the spring of 1906. Within three or four months it was dissolved after it had learned that its own constitution was so drafted as to make it a mere talking-shop and that the Tsar's privileges and rights as an autocratic monarch had all been carefullly preserved. The Paris Bourse and London Stock Exchange had absolved the Tsar from the necessity of keeping his promise of constitutional government given in the autumn of 1905.

At this point a new ambassador arrived from Britain, one of the most experienced and skilful of British diplomats who had been responsible for administering a snub to German ambitions at the Conference of Algeciras in the beginning of 1906.[4] It was Sir Arthur Nicolson's job to deal with Russia. By the end of May 1907 he was on the train to St Petersburg. It took fifteen months of tenuous and difficult negotiations. Then an understanding was reached and embodied in an Anglo-Russian convention signed on August 31, 1907, and often called 'The Partition of Persia'. The convention regarding Persia (now Iran) stated in its preamble that the two governments had "mutually agreed to respect the integrity and independence of Persia ... sincerely desiring the preservation of order throughout that country and its pacific development as well as the permanent establishment of equal opportunities for the commerce and industry of all other nations". Thereafter in view of the special interests which each empire possessed in Persia owing to their geographical and commercial situation they agreed in five detailed articles to carve up the country into British and Russian zones with a small neutral zone between the two – the Russians in the North and the British in the South.[5]

A second convention was about Afghanistan, where it was agreed that this mountainous country on the North West Frontier of India was "outside the sphere of influence" of Russia, which would enter into political relations with it only through the intermediary of His Britannic Majesty's Government, and that Russia would refrain from sending agents into Afghanistan.[6]

The third and last convention was regarding Tibet, where in the preamble it was stated that the two powers recognised the suzerain rights of China over Tibet, and that neither power would treat with Tibet except through the intermediary of the Chinese Government. Neither Government was to send a representative to Lhasa; and their interference, which had been particularly marked in the case of the invasion of Tibet in 1904 by General Younghusband, was henceforward to stop.

The conclusion in August 1907 of this Anglo-Russian Entente was followed by a state visit of His Britannic Majesty King Edward VII in June 1908 to the Gulf of Finland in the Royal Yacht the *Victoria and Albert* [7] with accompanying warships. The Tsar and his family were accompanied by their chief ministers and the King-Emperor by his leading admirals and generals. It was generally assumed that the cordial understanding was now developing into a military and naval alliance; certainly this was the assumption on the German side. A year later, in August 1909 Tsar Nicolas and his ministers and entourage voyaged to the Isle of Wight, there in the Roads, aboard the Royal ships, once more to meet and greet his affable uncle Edward VII. This was the stage reached in the effort to build up friendly relations between the British Empire and the Russian Empire.

But there were objections, at any rate on the British side, voiced in the House of Lords by Lord Curzon, the ex-Viceroy of India, who considered this Entente was harmful to the British Empire. This standpoint in some ways had been traditional in the Tory Party in the 19th century, while in contrast Liberal governments, particularly those of Palmerston and Gladstone, had on occasion made friendly gestures towards the Russian Empire – a matter to which Karl Marx drew attention again and again. There was however, amongst the mass of the British people, and even in the rank-and-file of the great swarming Liberal majority in the Parliament of 1906 to 1910, a strong objection to the rule of the Tsar, and hence to any intimate connection or friendship between the two empires. Keir Hardie had criticised the visit in summer 1908 of the King to the Tsar and he detailed the crimes of the Tsardom (3,205 political prisoners executed in two years and 6 times as many butchered by the Black Hundreds) in an article headed "Consorting with murderers". Both Keir Hardie and Arthur Henderson, then leader of the Labour Party, in the House of Commons denounced on July 22, 1909 the forthcoming visit of the Tsar; and their protest sufficed to prevent Nicholas II from actually setting foot on British soil. Underlying popular protest was a growing, if dim, suspicion that 'secret diplomacy' was at work.

But, protests not withstanding, the Anglo-Russian Entente was built up from 1906-07 onwards, particularly by the Liberal statesmen of British imperialism.

4 International socialism and the war danger

Outside British official circles which were busily endeavouring in these 7 years to transform 'friendly relations' into the close intimacies of a military alliance, there was this long-lasting objection to the Tsardom amongst the British people. In the organised sections of the British working-class this was evidenced nearly half a century earlier, when in 1864 the Inaugural Address of the First International concluded with denunciation of the "encroachments of that barbarous power whose head is at St Petersburg". This too was the outlook of the first socialist organisations of 1883 and after, and of the whole Socialist International, set up in 1889. When the Revolution in Russia of 1905-07 broke out, help was sent to the revolutionary socialists from Britain; and to the Labour Representation Committee there came a letter of thanks on behalf of the Russian Social-Democratic Labour Party. It was signed by Lenin.

In the same year (1907) that the Anglo-Russian Entente was signed, and in the same month, the 7th International Congress was meeting at Stuttgart. Realising the war danger, they passed a resolution in which, after confirming their standpoint "against militarism and imperialism", it was stated that:

> "The struggles against militarism cannot be separated from the socialist class struggle in general. Wars between capitalist states are, as a rule, the outcome of their competition on the world market, for each state seeks not only to secure its existing markets, but also to conquer new ones. In this, the subjugation of foreign peoples and countries plays a prominent role."

In the course of the same resolution it recalled that ever since the International Socialist Conference in Brussels in August 1891 the proletariat had tried out the most diverse ways for the purpose "of preventing the outbreak of wars or putting a stop to them, as well as for utilising the convulsions of society caused by war for the emancipation of the working class". Then, at the end of this 1907 resolution which laid down the policy of socialism on war, they set out an operative clause and in it made these stipulations as follows:

(1) On the threat of the outbreak of war "it is the duty of the working class in the countries involved" and of their representatives "to use every effort to prevent war".
(2) If nevertheless war were to break out "their duty is to intervene to bring it promptly to an end".
(3) and, with all their energies, to use the political and economic crisis created by the war to rouse the masses and thereby to hasten the downfall of capitalist class rule".

This was the proclaimed policy of socialism. This indeed, other than as a series of abstract propositions, was socialism in actuality, socialism as a policy, a doctrine and for many the equivalent to a faith.

From 1907 onward the danger of war grew greater year by year. In 1908 Austria-Hungary had annexed the one-time Balkan provinces of Bosnia-Herzegovina. This exacerbated the relations between the powers. According to a young British diplomat it meant that the Triple Alliance or at any rate the Central Empires "had succeeded in humiliating Russia, Serbia, France and England". In 1911, on July 1, there came the Agadir crisis caused by the dispatch of a German warship to a Moorish port. Reservists were mobilised to guard bridges in Kent and elsewhere near 'invasion ports'. Lloyd George, British Chancellor of the Exchequer, speaking to City bankers at the Mansion House on July 21, made it clear that the position of the British Government under certain circumstances was such that "I say emphatically that peace at that price would be intolerable for a great country like ours to endure." Not until the autumn was over did the risk of immediate outbreak recede.

On September 28, 1911, Italy declared war upon Turkey. Both France and Russia were bound by yet another secret treaty to raise no objection to Italy's attack on Turkey. Italy seized Tripoli and Cyrenaica and the islands of the Dodecanese in the Aegean.

The danger kept growing and in 1912 it became clear that the cauldron of the Balkans would soon be a-boil again. War alliances were rapidly being concluded. The Serbo-Bulgarian Treaty was signed on March 13, 1912. The Greco-Bulgarian Treaty was signed on May 9, 1912. On October 8, 1912, war was declared on Turkey by Montenegro, Serbia, Bulgaria and Greece. The danger of widening war was mounting. On December 3, the Turks asked for a ceasefire and delegates then met at St James' Palace in London to discuss terms of peace. Then the Balkan allies quarrelled over the spoils once the Treaty of London had been signed between Turkey and the Balkan states. On June 29, 1913, Bulgaria attacked Serbia. Greece and Rumania then turned together with Serbia upon Bulgaria. This was the second Balkan war which ended only some weeks later when, by a treaty signed in Bucharest on August 10, Serbia and Greece gained further territory at the expense of Bulgaria. These wars had been the summer lightning. They had prepared the way for war on a much greater scale.

There was no time to lose. Consequently as soon as the first Balkan war broke out in October 1912 the International Socialist Bureau called a special International Socialist Congress against imperialist war. It met in Basle, Switzerland, on November 24-25, 1912. The Manifesto of that Basle Congress confirmed the standpoint of international socialism which had been laid down at Stuttgart in 1907 and repeated at Copenhagen at the 8th International Congress in 1910. The *Manifesto* repeated the same operative clause and made certain other points of considerable significance. The Basle Manifesto stated:

"The Congress expects that the urban and rural proletariat of Russia, Finland and Poland, which is growing in strength, will destroy this web of lies, will oppose every belligerent venture of Tsarism, will combat every design of Tsarism whether upon Armenia or upon Constantinople, and will concentrate its whole force upon the renewal of the revolutionary struggle for emancipation from Tsarism. For Tsarism is the hope of all the reactionary powers in Europe, the most terrible enemy of the democracy of the peoples dominated by it; and the achievement of its destruction must be viewed as one of the foremost tasks of the entire International." *(25.xi.1912)*

The language was unmistakable. The closing sentences stated that:

"The proletariat is conscious at this moment of being the bearer of the entire future of mankind. The proletariat will exert all its energy to prevent the annihilation of the flower of all peoples, threatened by all the horrors of mass murders, starvation and pestilence."

Then came the final appeal:

"The Congress therefore appeals to you, proletarians and socialists of all countries, to make your voices heard in this decisive hour! Proclaim your will in every form and in all places; raise your protest in the Parliaments with all your force; unite in great mass demonstrations; use every means that the organisation and the strength of the proletariat place at your disposal! See to it that the governments are constantly kept aware of the vigilance and passionate will for peace on the part of the proletariat! To the capitalist world of exploitation and mass murder, oppose in this way the proletarian world of peace and fraternity of peoples." *(25.xi.1912)*

5 Attitude of Labour and Socialist Parties to the outbreak of war

In July 1914 the reiterated, thrice-ingeminated peace policy of international socialism was put to the test, first by the threat of war and then by its actual outbreak. The assassination in Sarajevo of the Archduke Franz Ferdinand on June 28, 1914, was followed a month later by Austria-Hungary declaring war against Serbia on Tuesday, July 28. Immediately the International Socialist Bureau met at Brussels. Unanimously they decided to hold straightaway, by August 9, an International Socialist Congress at Paris, and stated that:

"The Bureau considers it an obligation for the workers of all nations concerned, not only to continue, but even to strengthen, their demonstrations against war, in favour of peace, and of a settlement of the Austro-Serbian conflict by arbitration."

It was to be the last meeting that represented the whole International, the last meeting too of the Bureau that had been set up with such hopes in 1900. The Congress at Paris did not take place.

It remained for the national sections to carry out their international duty. The British Section of the Internationial Socialist Bureau was composed of 5 delegates from the Labour Party, 2 from the Independent Labour Party, 2 from the British Socialist Party, and one from the Fabian Society, together with the 3 British delegates to the Bureau. Of these last 3, two were appointed from a meeting of the British delegation 4 years earlier at the Copenhagen International Socialist Congress, while the third was elected by members of the Labour Party in the House of Commons. The secretary of the British Section was Arthur Henderson, secretary of the Labour Party. The 3 British delegates to the Bureau were Keir Hardie, Dan Irving and Ramsay MacDonald MP.

In Britain, on Saturday, August 1, 1914, the British Section of the International Socialist Bureau issued its manifesto over the joint signatures of Keir Hardie and Arthur Henderson:

MANIFESTO TO THE BRITISH PEOPLE

The long-threatened European war is now upon us. For more than 100 years no such danger has confronted civilisation. It is for you to take full account of the desperate situation and to act promptly and vigorously in the interest of peace. You have never been consulted about the war.

Whatever may be the rights and wrongs of the sudden crushing attack made by the militarist Empire of Austria upon Servia, it is certain that the workers of all countries likely to be drawn into the conflict must strain every nerve to prevent their governments from committing them to war.

Everywhere socialists and the organised forces of Labour are taking this course. Everywhere vehement protests are made against the greed and intrigues of militarists and armament-mongers.

We call upon you to do the same here in Great Britain upon an even more impressive scale. Hold vast demonstrations against war in every industrial centre. Compel those of the governing class and their press who are eager to commit you to co-operate with Russian despotism to keep silence, and respect the decision of the overwhelming majority of the people, who will have neither part nor lot in such infamy. The success of Russia at the present day would be a curse to the world.

There is no time to lose. Already, by secret agreements and understandings, of which the democracies of the civilised world know only by rumour, steps are being taken which may fling us all into the fray.

Workers, stand together, therefore, for peace! Combine and conquer the militarist enemy and the self-seeking imperialists today, once and for all.

Men and women of Britain, you have now an unexampled opportunity of rendering a magnificent service to humanity, and to the world!

Proclaim that for you the days of plunder and butchery have gone by. Send messages of peace and fraternity to your fellows who have less liberty than you. Down with class rule! Down with the rule of brute force! Down with war! Up with the peaceful rule of the people!

On Sunday, August 2, 1914, a great demonstration, representative of all sections of the working class, was held in Trafalgar Square under the auspices of the British Section. Both Keir Hardie and Arthur Henderson were amongst the speakers and these included the finest orator of them all, R B Cunninghame Graham, one of the original members of the International Socialist Congress in 1889 and the first Member of Parliament to proclaim himself a socialist, nearly 30 years earlier. The following resolution was carried:

> "That this demonstration, representing the organised workers and citizens of London, views with serious alarm the prospects of a European war, into which every European power will be dragged owing to secret alliances and understandings which in their origin were never sanctioned by the nations, nor are even now communicated to them;
>
> "We stand by the efforts of the international working-class movement to unite workers of the nations concerned in their efforts to prevent their governments from entering upon war, as expressed in the resolution passed by the International Socialist Bureau;
>
> "We protest against any step being taken by the Government of this country to support Russia, either directly or in consequence of any understanding with France, as being not only offensive to the political traditions of the country but disastrous to Europe;
>
> "And declare that, as we have no interest, direct or indirect, in the threatened quarrels which may result from the action of Austria in Servia, the Government of Great Britain should rigidly decline to engage in war, but should confine itself to efforts to bring about peace as speedily as possible."
> (2.viii.1914)

These were strong words. They showed all constituents of the British Section of the International Socialist Bureau were united in their desire and their efforts for the prevention of war. They were carrying out the first part of declared socialist policy as thrice set forth in the International Socialist Congresses of 1907 and 1910 and 1912.

The attempt failed. They were unable to prevent the outbreak. Two days later, on August 4, 1914, Britain declared war on Germany.

Within a week the situation was entirely different and so was the standpoint of the members of the British Section of the International Socialist Bureau. They had altered their positions. They were supporting their own government. So far from intervening "to bring it promptly to an end" they were joining in a recruiting campaign together with the capitalist parties. The overwhelming majority of the Labour movement abandoned its previous standpoint and swung in behind the government.

The same was the case in every belligerent country with only a few exceptions (the parties in Russia and Serbia and minorities elsewhere). The Russian Bolsheviks and the Social-Democratic Party of Serbia remained true to international socialism and to its policy and standpoint. But at the outset they were alone. Yet the leaders of all parties had subscribed and signed their names to the Basle Manifesto. In the course of the 6 months that followed any hesitations disappeared. The trade unions of Britain, the Trades Union Congress Parliamentary Committee, the Parliamentary Labour Party became supporters of the war against Germany, and in most cases became out-and-out jingoes. In each country there was a very small minority who continued to maintain the standpoint of international socialism. In Britain the Independent Labour Party had an anti-war standpoint. Their manifesto, published on August 13, 1914, contained such phrases as:

> "Out of the darkness and the depth we hail our working-class comrades of every land. Across the roar of guns, we send sympathy and greeting to the German Socialists. They have laboured unceasingly to promote good relations with Britain, as we with Germany. They are no enemies of ours but faithful friends."

Words of sanity like these were to become rare in the autumn of 1914 and were soon unheard amid the roaring torrent of jingoism.

6   The Stockholm Project

By the beginning of the year 1917, after 30 months of the war, there was a longing for peace in every country of Europe. But no ending to the war seemed in sight when suddenly the Russian Revolution brought a new aspect in mid-March 1917 to international working-class relations. 8 weeks later, when the policy of Lenin's *April Theses* came before the 7th Conference of the Russian Social-Democratic Labour Party (Bolsheviks), the Executive Committee of the Petrograd Soviet (then mainly made up of Mensheviks and SRs) hastily put forward a rival policy. On May 9 they launched a summons for an International Socialist Conference, to be held at

Stockholm. This became known as the Stockholm Project.

On May 1 Foreign Minister Paul Milyukov had issued a Note declaring adherence to the treaties with the Allies. This brought strong representations from the workers' organisations, which demanded a change of government.

On May 15 Milyukov resigned his post as Foreign Minister, owing to strong protest demonstrations. The first Provisional Government was toppled over; and the second, a coalition Provisional Government was formed on May 18, under the same Prince Lvov but with Kerensky as War Minister

Meantime, such a call as that issued on May 9 was bound to arouse a response and to awaken the slumbering socialist aspirations. By May 28 the French Socialist Party had decided in favour of the Stockholm Project. By June 3 a Convention to form a Workers' and Soldiers' Council had been held in Leeds, and this also welcomed the Stockholm Project.

The British and French Governments were at first prepared to consider the proposal in order to meet what might seem to be the wishes of their Russian ally but later began to dread its effect on their war aims. In the first stage the decision was taken that Arthur Henderson, Secretary of the Labour Party and one of the 5 members of the War Cabinet, should travel to Petrograd and see what he could do. He had full power if need be to remove Sir George Buchanan and himself assume the post of Ambassador with plenipotentiary powers. Henderson went off to Russia on May 25 and returned on June 24, 1917.

Henderson spent just one month in Petrograd and returned without having accomplished what the British Government had hoped from his presence, but was himself considerably affected by what he had found in Russia and in Petrograd. For if Arthur Henderson had made little impact, the Petrograd Soviet had made a big impression on him. Henderson carried through his mission, took the decision that the embassy should remain in the hands of Sir George Buchanan (who was fulsomely grateful for this concession) and returned convinced that it was necessary to support the idea of the Stockholm conference. He believed that this would help the British Government and eventually the Labour Party, of which he was the head. Consequently, on his return around mid-summer, Arthur Henderson arranged for a special conference of the British Labour Party to be held on August 10.[8]

This was the first organisational impact of the Russian Revolution on the British Labour movement. There was, however, from this point onwards the development not only of the previous division between the pro-war and the anti-war sections of the Labour movement, but on the one hand an extreme Right-wing began to develop and on the other hand a true Left began to emerge, mainly in the workshops.

At the conference on August 10 the Labour Party decided to support the Stockholm Project by 1,840,0000 to 550,000 votes. This put the fat in the fire. A meeting of 4 of the 5 members of the War Cabinet the next day forced Henderson's resignation. Actually they refused to allow Henderson into the room in which they were sitting until they had made their decision. It was a slap in the face. It was a sudden reassertion on the part of the Leader of the Tory Party, of the Leader of the House of Lords and of the Prime Minister that they represented the ruling class and that Labour must learn to keep its place. This treatment of the revered Arthur Henderson, Leader of the Labour Party and lay preacher of the Methodist Church, was to have many repercussions. In the papers it was described as Henderson being left standing "on the mat" outside the door of the Cabinet Room. The effect was discussed, talked of in practically every trade union branch and in the workshops in the country. Great publicity was given to it.

This did not, however, mean that Henderson representing the majority of the Labour Party had altered in any way his general support of the government's prosecution of the war. This was seen when it was agreed that the Labour Party should continue in the Coalition with other ministers to take the place of Henderson. Consequently on August 14 the Rt Hon G N Barnes, once Leader of the Labour Party in the brief session of 1910, succeeded to Henderson's War Cabinet seat which had been kept warm for him during Henderson's absence in Russia. On August 17, the Rt Hon John Hodge became Minister of Pensions; G H Roberts became Minister of Labour; G J Wardle became Parliamentary Secretary to the Board of Trade.

But the matter was not a personal one. A further conference of the Labour Party on August 21, 1917 confirmed this. There, however, the weight of those who accepted the standpoint of Lloyd George proved strong enough to diminish considerably the majority in favour of Stockholm. It was only by a 3,000 majority that the Labour conference reaffirmed the decision that they would send delegates to the international peace conference. But how junior a partner the Labour Party was in the coalition government was immediately shown by the fact that passports to enable this conference decision to be carried out were refused to the delegates.

The repercussions of the tiff with the War Cabinet were considerable. Henderson and the trade union leaders within the Labour Party began to move in the direction of organisational independence. On August 26 a Labour Party sub-committee was appointed to prepare a scheme of reorganisation of the party. This, as it turned out, was to entail not only reorganisation of the party in such a way as to put it partly on a basis of individual membership, supplementary to the corporate affiliations which hitherto had been all its constituents, but was also to result in the preparation of an effective electoral fighting machine. Labour was going to assert itself and to claim more seats than the mere two score of mainly trade union MPs out of the 670 which hitherto had been its portion in Parliament. Actually the number of Labour Members was more than doubled in the next general election, trebled and quadrupled at the general elections of successive years, until the advent of the first Labout Government in 1924. It was not only a plan for party reorganisation, it was in a sense the recreation of an independent political organisation.

What had begun as the Labour Representation Committee in 1900, reinforced by a number of MPs from affiliated unions who personally were for the most part Liberals in their outlook, had not fulfilled the somewhat rosy hopes of its founders. Not only had there never been a socialist programme, but the programme of independent representation in Parliament, under the cover of whatever formalities, was seriously sapped in the years 1906 to 1914, and especially from 1910 to 1914, by the firm adherence of Labour Party MPs to the policies of the Liberal government. This had been intensifed during the first year of hostilities, and thereafter sealed by the inclusion of Labour Party leaders in the coalition governments of May 1915 and December 1916. The Labour Party Members of Parliament could be counted upon as members and supporters of the coalition rather than as independent Members of Parliament.

The impact of the Revolution brought about these happenings of August 1917 which, in turn, set afoot a new process. It was decided to have a programme; and, further, that the programme should be broadly, very broadly, socialist. Consequently throughout the autumn and early winter of 1917, a group headed by Sidney Webb and Arthur Henderson was elaborating both a new constitution and, for the first time, a socialist programme for the Labour Party. The quality of the socialism, the kind of socialism, is not the question here.

The effect of the October Revolution, when the Russian Revolution reached its second and triumphant stage, made it seem still more urgent to redefine the position of the Labour Party and to have a new constitution. Consequently, to anticipate the next chapter, it can be said here that on January 23, 1918, a Labour Party conference was held at Nottingham. This was followed by an inter-Allied socialist conference on war aims in London on February 20, 1918. All this led up to the new Labour Party constitution, adopted at a special conference on February 26, 1918.

Notes and References

1   Eg, "Let us complain to them what fools were here.
    Disguised like Muscovites, in shapeless gear"
    (*Love's Labour's Lost*)
2   F Engels, *Letter to Marx*, 7 October 1858, in K Marx and F Engels, *Collected Works*, Vol 40, p 344 –Ed.
3   Hence the poet Tennyson's anti-democratic outburst in 1886, when he was troubled both by the vote being given to agricultural labourers in the Reform Act of 1884, and by the Pendjeh incident on the Afghan frontier.
        "Russia bursts our Indian barrier, shall we fight her? Shall we yield?
        Pause! before you sound the trumpet, hear the voices from the field.
        Those three hundred millions under one Imperial sceptre now,
        Shall we hold them? Shall we loose them? Take the suffrage of the plough."
4   The Act of Algeciras had been signed by 10 powers of Europe. It was the Concert of Europe plus the United States of America, now brought in for the first time and admitted to the magic circle.
5   Of these two zones the Russian was considerably the larger with Teheran included, and as it seemed at first glance the more fertile; but beyond the British zone, and nearly accessible from the Persian Gulf (though in the neutral zone) were rich oil fields, soon to be exploited by the Anglo-Persian Oil Company – which now

after many developments uses the name in this country of British Petroleum.

6   This convention was made without the consent of the Emir of Afghanistan who never gave his consent to this disposal of his country's affairs. The preamble, however, stated these steps were to be taken "in order to assure perfect security on the respective frontiers of Central Asia and the maintenance on those regions of permanent peace".

7   This was the third of the same name, launched in 1899.

8   As to the impact *on* Henderson, it was remarked at the time to the author by W Stephen Sanders, who had been secretary of the Fabian Society, that "Arthur Henderson, the old, highly respected chief layman of the Methodist Church, with his background of Liberalism and of friendly society type of trade unionism, could hardly be expected to exercise any influence upon the groups of Jewish atheists who led the socialists in Petrograd."

Appendix I

The makeup of the British Section of the Second International

In Britain and Russia alike the first socialist groupings dated from the early '80s of last century. In Britain these were: the Social-Democratic Federation, headed by Hyndman (1883); the Fabian Society, headed by Bernard Shaw and Sidney Webb (1884); the Socialist League, headed by William Morris (1884) – which lasted only for a few years. Ten years later, in 1893, there came the Independent Labour Party, headed by Keir Hardie. In February 1900 these three bodies linked up with some three dozen trade unions to form an electoral alliance called the Labour Representation Committee, which had its first big success in January 1906 when 29 of its candidates were elected. The Committee thereafter called itself the Labour Party.

Also in 1900 there was set up an International Socialist Bureau, to which these three organisations from Britain affiliated. In 1908 the proposal was made that the Labour Party also should be affiliated, although it had as yet no individual membership, no socialist programme, indeed, no general programme at all. Affiliation to the International Socialist Bureau was open to:

1. "All associations which adhere to the essential principles of socialism: socialisation of the means of production and distribution; international union and action of the workers; conquest of public powers by the proletariat organised as a class party.

2. "All the constituted organisations which accept the principle of a class struggle and recognise the necessity for political action (legislative and Parliamentary), but do not participate directly in the political movement."

These conditions were drawn up following the London International Socialist Congress of 1896 in order to exclude anarchists, and to admit trade unions and other labour organisations which, although agreeing with political action, were not definitely political in character.

The application of the Labour Party to be affiliated raised the question of definition. The International Socialist Bureau, at its meeting in Brussels on Sunday, October 11, 1908, which was attended by Lenin,[1] decided by a big majority to accept the Labour Party on the motion of Karl Kautsky:

"Whereas by previous resolutions of the International Congresses, all organisations adopting the standpoint of the proletarian class struggle and recognising the necessity for political action have been accepted for membership, the International Bureau declares that the British Labour Party is admitted to International Socialist Congresses because, whilst not expressly accepting the proletarian class struggle, in practice the Labour Party conducts this struggle, and adopts its standpoint, inasmuch as the party is organised independently of the bourgeois parties."

Lenin held the view that

"the British trade unions, insular, aristocratic, philistinely selfish, and hostile to socialism, which have produced a number of outright traitors to the working class who have sold themselves to the bourgeoisie for ministerial posts (like the scoundrel John Burns), have nevertheless begun *moving towards* socialism, awkwardly, inconsistently, in zigzag fashion, but still moving towards socialism."[2]

Notes and References

1   Lenin associated himself with Kautsky's resolution against the standpoint of Hyndman who wished the Labour Party to be rejected, but he proposed an amendment, which was not accepted, that the last part of the resolution should run as follows: "because it represents the first step on the part of the really proletarian organisations of Britain towards a conscious class policy and towards a *socialist* workers' party."

2   Lenin, *Meeting of the International Socialist Bureau*, in *Collected Works*, Vol 15, p 237 *–Ed.*

Appendix II

Zimmerwald and the Independent Labour Party

The ILP at the outset of the war lost a number of their leading members who held high positions in the trade unions. On the other hand as the war developed it gained more and more members. The signs of 'war weariness' multiplied with the rise in casualties; the tightening restrictions upon civil rights and liberties by the Defence of the Realm Act with its Orders-in-Council and its crushing Regulations under Order-in-Council; and from March 1916 onwards with conscription of an increasingly severe nature imposed by the Military Service Acts. Amongst the new members some were pacifists who found in the ILP the only political party that would express their point of view, while others were Quakers from the Society of Friends, whose Christian pacifist outlook was well known. There was a considerable swing towards pacifism.

When the International Socialist Conference met at Zimmerwald in Switzerland on September 5-8, 1915, the ILP was ready to participate. The ILP delegates, however, were refused passports. The Manifesto stated that not only the individual socialist parties but the highest representative body, the International Socialist Bureau, had failed the working class. Then it explained why they had met in neutral Switzerland, as follows:

> "In this unbearable situation, we, representatives of the socialist parties, trade unions and their minorities, we Germans, French, Italians, Russians, Poles, Letts, Romanians, Bulgarians, Swedes, Norwegians, Dutch and Swiss, we who stand not on the ground of national solidarity with the exploiting class, but on the ground of the international solidarity of the proletariat and of the class struggle, have assembled to re-tie the torn threads of international relations and to call upon the working class to recover itself and to fight for peace."

Then came the call to struggle beginning with the words:

> "Proletarians;
> "Since the outbreak of the war, you have placed your energy, your courage, your endurance at the service of the ruling classes. Now you must stand up for your own cause, for the sacred aims of socialism, for the emancipation of the oppressed nations as well as of the enslaved classes, by means of the irreconcilable proletarian class struggle.
> "It is the task and the duty of the socialists of the belligerent countries to take up this struggle with full force; it is the task and the duty of the socialists of

the neutral states to support their brothers in this struggle against bloody barbarism with every effective means."

This Manifesto was signed by representatives of 10 delegations, including Lenin.

There was also a draft resolution drawn up by Left-wing delegates at the International Socialist Conference at Zimmerwald. This contained statements which the majority had not been willing to accept, and it was submitted to the International Socialist Commission at Berne and appeared in its Bulletin No 2 of November 27, 1915. This was signed on behalf of the Central Committee of the Russian Social-Democratic Labour Party by Zinoviev and Lenin; by Radek, representing the opposition of the Polish Social Democracy; by Winter (Jan Berzin), a representative of the Latvian province; and by 4 other delegates, one of them German and the other 3 from neutral countries. On the question of submitting the draft to the Commission, 12 delegates voted in favour, namely these 8 signatories to the draft plus Trotsky and Roland-Holst and two Socialist-Revolutionists, of Holland.

TWO DECLARATIONS MADE AT THE INTERNATIONAL SOCIALIST CONFERENCE AT ZIMMERWALD

"The undersigned declare as follows:

"The Manifesto adopted by the conference does not give us complete satisfaction. It contains no pronouncement upon either open opportunism, or opportunism that is hiding under radical phraseology – the opportunism which is not only the chief cause of the collapse of the International, but which strives to perpetuate that collapse. The Manifesto contains no clear pronouncement as to the methods of fighting against the war.

"We shall continue, as we have done heretofore, to advocate in the socialist press and at the meetings of International, a clear-cut Marxian position in regard to the tasks with which the epoch of imperialism has confronted the proletariat.

"We vote for the manifesto because we regard it as a call to struggle, and in this struggle we are anxious to march side by side with the other sections of the International.

We request that our present declaration be included in the official proceedings."

Signed: N Lenin, G Zinoviev, Radek, Nerman, Hoeglund and Winter.

The other declaration, which was signed, in addition to the group that had introduced the resolution of the Left, by Roland-Holst and Trotsky, read as follows: "Inasmuch as the adoption of our amendment (to the Manifesto) demanding the vote against war appropriations might in a way endanger the success of the conference, we do, under protests withdraw our amendment and accept Ledebour's statement in the commission to the effect that the Manifesto contains all that is implied in our proposition."

It may be added that Ledebour, as an ultimatum, demanded the rejection of the amendment, refusing to sign the Manifesto otherwise. (*Sotsial-Demokrat*, No 47, October 13, 1915)

The ILP, though unable to attend, declared its solidarity with the Zimmerwald Manifesto. The subsequent conference held in spring 1916, at Kienthal, had a bigger vote for the Zimmerwald Left than at Zimmerwald itself, but still they did not have a majority. The Zimmerwald Left was afterwards to be regarded as a step towards the creation of a new International.

Whether the ILP was fully aware of the standpoint of the Zimmerwald Left may be uncertain. But their subsequent attitude makes it unlikely that they had gone beyond the standpoint of the Zimmerwald majority. In 1916 there was a concentration against the Military Service Acts headed by the No-Conscription Fellowship whose leading officials were most leading members of the ILP.

Thus when April 1916 was marked by the Easter Rising in Ireland the ILP did not take up an anti-imperialist attitude that could rank it with the Zimmerwald Left.[1]

Notes and References

1   Here may be quoted a postscript written by Lenin to his article of October 1916, entitled *The Disarmament Slogan*, as follows:
    "PS. In the last issue of the English *Socialist Review* (September 1916), organ of the opportunist Independent Labour Party, we find, on page 287, the resolution of the party's Newcastle Conference – refusal to support any war waged by any government even if 'nominally' it is a war of 'defence'. And in an editorial on page 205 of the same issue we read the following declaration:
    'In no degree do we approve the Sinn Fein rebellion. We do not approve armed rebellion at all, any more than any other form of militarism and war.'
    "Is there any need to prove that *these* 'anti-militarists', that *such* advocates of disarmament, not in a small, but in a big country, are the most pernicious opportunists? And yet, theoretically, they are quite right in regarding insurrection as one "form" of militarism and war." (Lenin, *Collected Works*, Vol 23, p 104)

Appendix III

The United Socialist Council

The great event of the fourth week of April 1916 was the Easter Rising in Ireland. The Sinn Fein rebellion for many in Britain was to be a precursor of the turmoil stirred by the impact of the Russian Revolution eleven months later. That same Easter the conference of the British Socialist Party overwhelmingly decided against Hyndman and other pro-war leaders. It reverted to the policy of the pre-war Socialist International and also stood for the policy of Zimmerwald. Thus, of the socialist constituents of the British Section of the International Socialist Bureau, two out of the three had now pronounced against support of the imperialist war.[1] The way was open for joint anti-war activity, and a United Socialist Council came into being, composed as follows: 4 representatives each from the ILP and the BSP, namely; for the ILP, W C Anderson MP, F W Jowett, Ramsay MacDonald MP and Philip Snowden MP; for the BSP, H Alexander, E C Fairchild, A A Watts and Fred Shaw. The joint secretaries were Francis Johnson and Albert Inkpin.

The United Socialist Council had both the weeklies the *Labour Leader* and *The Call* as organs of their developing standpoint. But they were also able to call upon the help of the weekly *Herald*, the circulation of which was reckoned to be greater than either of the other weeklies, while its editor, George Lansbury, had in his time been a prominent leader first of the Social-Democratic Federation and later of the Independent Labour Party. The United Socialist Council through its two constituents could however have only the influence of a small minority upon the Labour Party which was completely pro-war and indeed was represented from May 1915 onwards in the war-time coalition, first under Asquith and then under Lloyd George.

In the spring of 1917 and the early summer there was launched an appeal for a general convention to welcome the Russian Revolution and to take practical steps in its vindication. The *Herald* campaigned for such a convention and was instrumental in securing for its chairmanship no other than Robert Smillie, the beloved President of the Miners' Federation of Great Britain. The four MPs of the Independent Labour Party had singularly little influence at that time on the body of the Labour Party, and indeed were more or less ostracised by their fellow Members of Parliament. There was no representative of the BSP at all in the legislature, as the only Members of Parliament who held their view had seceded along with Hyndman, who then formed a National Socialist Party in June 1916. But the securing of the aid of Robert Smilllie alone seemed to guarantee that many local and national trade union leaders would respond to the summons to welcome the Russian Revolution.

The convention was a great success and roused expectations everywhere, not only amongst the nearly 1200 delegates, but in the various towns and in all sections of the labour movement where there was any degree of anti-war feeling which, insofar as it was not pacifist, was almost by definition bound to welcome revolution and revolutionary action. Many of the delegates were from the Shop Stewards' movement, including William Gallacher, from the Clyde Workers' Committee, released from prison only a few weeks before. Ernest Bevin, at that time a Left-wing organiser of the dock workers on the Bristol Channel, also came. Many speeches were made asking that a call for peace should be sent from the conference, and a resolution was passed proposing that councils of workmen's and soldiers' delegates should be formed in Britain, both to support the Russian Revolution and to work for peace. Tom Quelch, son of the famous Harry Quelch, was appointed organiser and a provisional executive was appointed.

Councils sprang up here and there. But they were not of the quality or the kind that could imitate effectively the correspondingly named bodies that had sprung up in Petrograd and other towns of Russia. There was not yet a revolutionary situation in Britain nor were there the potentialities in the existing parties to operate in such a situation if it had existed. Thus the great conference at Leeds on June 1, so far from going from strength to strength with district and local British councils of workmen and soldiers, was presently watered down. In October the provisional committee, with three of the Independent Labour Party Members of Parliament upon it, accepted a decision that the councils should be regarded as propagandist bodies and not as rivals to existing working-class organisations.

This first endeavour to 'cash in' on the response and welcome given to the Russian Revolution, in order to create corresponding revolutionary bodies in Britain, turned out to be a flash in the pan. On the other hand they were able to do much as part of a Hands off Russia movement to defend the Russian Revolution in general during the first 12 months after March and November 1917. Both the ILP and the BSP from this time onwards responded to the call of the Russian Revolution by printing translations of Lenin's writings and circulating these in the workshops as pamphlets, while at the same time they spread leaflets throughout the country. Such then was the impact in 1917 of the Russian Revolution.

Notes and References

1   The third constituent, the Fabian Society, had made no pronouncement, but in meetings of the British Section of the Bureau its representatives sided with the pro-war majority – which did not prevent the existence of a small section who were anti-war and in favour of the standpoint of international socialism – especially amongst the younger members.

Appendix IV

The Stockholm Project, the Labour Party and the War Cabinet

The Stockholm Project was part of the impact of the Russian Revolution upon the political parties as well as the peoples of the belligerent powers, both of the enemy powers and of the Allies. This May 9 proposal of the Petrograd Soviet, launched at an early stage when the Bolshevik members were still in a small minority, caused a flutter in the dovecotes. This project for a conference of socialists of every hue caused some disarray in the government as well as in the Labour movement of the United Kingdom. At the outset there was a disposition to look upon it favourably; but only a few weeks elapsed before the project became suspect. The other proposal which had been put forward by the Russian Government for a Conference of the Allies seemed acceptable provided it was postponed, was limited in its purposes and did not prematurely raise the question of the treaties that embodied the war aims. Both these questions were anxiously discussed in the British War Cabinet. Stockholm alone with its repercussions occupied much of the time of the War Cabinet from mid-July to mid-August 1917, as is evidenced in their minutes, recently made available for public inspection. For example, following some anxious discussion on these matters:

"The War Cabinet were agreed that:

(a) In the present state of the War it was desirable to postpone the discussion of War Aims as long as possible, as, once it was known that we were discussing these questions, the effective prosecution of the war might be rendered more difficult. For this reason it was important to discourage the idea that this subject would be discussed at the next conference, and the Secretary of State for Foreign Affairs should adopt this attitude in replying to any queries he might receive from the representatives of the various Powers." *(Monday, 16.vii.1917)*

At the same time it was agreed that:

"(b) A decision as to the subjects for discussion by, and the date of, the proposed Conference on the Revision of Treaties, should be deferred until the return of Mr Arthur Henderson from Russia."

Ten days later the vexed question comes up again under the rubric "Allied Socialist Conference" in *WC 196(16)* as follows:

"With reference to a Foreign Office telegram from Mr G M Young, through Lord Bertie, and a telegram from Mr Arthur Henderson, Lord Robert Cecil raised the question of issuing passports to the Right Hon Arthur Henderson, MP, Mr Wardle, MP, and Mr Ramsay Macdonald, MP, to enable them to proceed to Paris on 27th July accompanied by four Russian Soviet delegates, in order to confer with the French Socialists regarding:
(a) The proposed Allied Socialist Conference in London on 8th and 9th August;
(b) An International Socialist Conference at Stockholm early in September. He pointed out that the Italian Government had reaffirmed their objection to allowing representatives to attend the latter, and it was decided that –

Mr Henderson should be asked to confer with his colleagues in the War Cabinet at 7.30 pm that evening, with a view to their ascertaining from him how far the proposed action
(1) Committed His Majesty's Government to assent to British Socialist representatives meeting enemy Socialist representatives at Stockholm;
(2) Whether the inclusion of Mr Ramsay MacDonald, MP, among those to be allowed to proceed to Paris implied official recognition by the British Government of Mr Ramsay MacDonald's status as a representative of British Socialists."
(Initialled)   ABL
2 Whitehall Gardens, SW
July 26, 1917.

Six days later, at 4.30 in the afternoon, came the famous meeting of the War Cabinet at 10 Downing Street at which the leader of the Labour Party was kept 'on the doormat' while his colleagues debated what to do with him. Present were the Prime Minister, in the Chair, and the following dignitaries:

The Right Hon the Earl Curzon of Kedleston, KG, GCSI, GCIE.
The Right Hon the Viscount Milner, GCB, GCMG.
The Right Hon A Bonar Law, MP.
The Right Hon Sir E Carson, KC, MP.

The following were also present:

The Right Hon A J Balfour, OM, MP, Secretary of State for Foreign
    Affairs.
The Right Hon W Long, MP, Secretary of State for the Colonies.
Lieutenant-Colonel Sir M P A Hankey, KCB, Secretary.

Apparently G N Barnes MP, once a secretary to Tom Mann and one-time general secretary of the Amalgamated Society of Engineers, had also been present at the private discussion. At any rate Barnes was scheduled to be the cuckoo in the Cabinet nest. The minute of the famous meeting with the rubric "Mr Arthur Henderson's visit to Paris: The Stockholm Conference" begins as follows:

> "PRIOR to Mr Henderson's arrival, the other members of the War Cabinet discussed the question among themselves, in continuation of the meeting held on the same morning (War Cabinet 201A). Mr. Henderson demurred to this procedure, as he was invited to attend at 4.30 and had waited one hour, and even then was not invited into the Cabinet, but it was explained that it had been adopted with special regard to Mr Henderson's interest and feelings, and that no slight had been intended. There was some discussion as to the nature of the answers which had been given in the House of Commons to questions in regard to Mr Henderson's visit to Paris. Mr Henderson considered that these had given a somewhat misleading impression of the whole transaction, more especially because they omitted all reference to the discussion that had taken place at the War Cabinet on the afternoon of Thursday, the 26th July. He pointed out that this had been particularly marked in the abbreviated versions that had been telegraphed to Paris, and these had given rise to considerable comment among the French.
>
> Mr Henderson reminded the War Cabinet that the question of the Stockholm Conference had never been discussed by those who were specially entitled to a view in the matter, namely, the Allied Socialist Parties. The proposal had originally been made by the Russian Soldiers' and Workmen's Committee without conference with their Allies. The policy of the British Labour Party towards it had been to postpone it as long as possible; in fact, they had adopted precisely the same attitude towards it as that of the Government towards the Russian Government's proposals for a Government Conference on War Aims." *(WC 202, Wednesday, 1.viii.1917)*

Then there followed Arthur Henderson's speech to his colleagues, which was very fully minuted as though the notetaker had realised not only the gravity of the breach in Cabinet solidarity but that the 'exculpation', if any, should be accorded unusual length. Today it reads oddly; but it has to be remembered that the long summer afternoon at the English country house had vanished only three years earlier; and that it was possible to recall days when an erring head of the servants' hall might be called upon to provide explanation and 'justification' of his action.

"Mr Henderson recalled that, before he had left England, the War Cabinet themselves had agreed that if a Conference at Stockholm was held at all it would be advisable that British representatives should be present *(War Cabinet 141, Minute 15)*. Circumstances had, he admitted, changed considerably since then, but until he met his colleagues he had no information that their attitude on the subject had changed.

He himself had returned from Petrograd somewhat under the influence of the daily discussions he had had with the Russian Foreign Secretary, who had insisted very strongly, and almost up to the moment of his departure, on the great importance that the Russian Government attached to the holding of the Stockholm Conference as a means of clearing away the suspicions that existed in Russia of British Imperialistic designs. The Russian Government had wished the Stockholm Conference to precede the Government Conference on War Aims, their reason being that an Allied Socialist Conference, as proposed by the British Labour Party, would not exercise any influence on the Governments concerned, whereas they considered that the Stockholm Conference would.

Owing to the inability of the British Government to send a warship to bring him back from Norway, Mr Henderson said that he had been delayed three or four days on his journey, with the result that the Prime Minister had left for Paris before he reached London. On his arrival he had found himself confronted with an invitation from the French Socialists to the Russian Socialists and the British Labour Party to proceed at once to Paris to discuss the Allied Socialist Conference and the Stockholm Conference. Before he had met his colleagues in the War Cabinet, he had had to attend a meeting of the British Labour Party's Executive, and at this meeting it had been decided to accept the invitation of the French Socialists and to proceed to Paris, and Mr Henderson himself, as Secretary of the British Labour Party's Executive, together with Mr Ramsay MacDonald, the Treasurer, and Mr Wardle had been selected as representatives. Immediately this decision was reached, he had telegraphed it direct to the Prime Minister at Paris, and on the afternoon of the following day he had met his colleagues and frankly discussed the whole question with them at the War Cabinet.

Mr Henderson justifed his acceptance of a nomination to go to Paris by pointing out that, as the Russian Socialists had accepted, it was eminently desirable that British representatives should also attend. Further, as Mr Ramsay Macdonald, as Treasurer of the British Labour Party's Executive, was selected, it was desirable that those who held different views from him should be represented.[1]

At Paris the Stockholm Conference had been discussed as a matter that was already settled in principle, and Mr Henderson himself had taken the line which he had decided on his return from Russia to be best calculated to promote the national interests, that is to say:

1. To postpone the Stockholm Conference as long as possible.
2. To do his utmost to ensure that it should not be a Conference to take decisions, but merely a consultation at which the British and French delegates could expound the British and French case.

At Paris he had stood out against the Russian and French Socialists for this point of view. The French had wished the Socialist parties of the various nations to be bound by the decisions of the Conference, because they had thought that by these means they could secure French aims in regard to Alsace and Lorraine. He himself, however, had explained that Great Britain was confronted with special difficulties in the matter of war aims, and that the British Labour Party could not permit themselves to be bound by the decisions of the Conference. He had stated that he would have to reconsider his position in regard to the Conference if he found the resolutions were to be binding and eventually he had succeeded in securing the adoption of his point of view. He had also succeeded in obtaining the postponement of the Conference from August 15 to September 10 in order to give time for the representative of the United States Labour Party to attend the Allied Conference that was to precede the Stockholm Conference." *(WC 202, 1.viii.1917)*

It is not necessary to follow the agonies of the War Cabinet day by day as Stockholm still came up on their agenda. On the question whether the government should allow British delegates to go to Stockholm the War Cabinet were agreed that "since May *(War Cabinet 151, minute 15)*, when our main object was to sustain the Russian Government, decisive changes had taken place". To them it was now clear that "The influence of the Soviet in Russia was steadily declining, and that the attendance of the British delegates in Stockholm was less important than formerly". *(Wednesday, 8.viii.1917)* From their point of view the best course appeared to be to leave the final decision until after the meeting of the Labour Party on Friday August 10. Meanwhile, in reply to questions in the House of Commons, Bonar Law should state that the attendance of British delegates at Stockholm "would be illegal".

On Friday August 10 at 6.15 in the evening there was an anxious meeting of the quinquevirate in 10 Downing Street – without Arthur Henderson. But they had a shorthand note of his speech delivered earlier that day and it made them very angry. For, following on it, the Labour Party Conference had cast 1,846,000 votes against 550,000, in favour of representation at the Stockholm Conference. Thereupon the War Cabinet decided "Not to permit British Representation at the Conference."

Under the strange rubric "Mr Arthur Henderson's attitude" the minutes recount that "the discussion centred mainly on Mr Arthur Henderson's speech". They thought it had been "misleading", particularly since "no mention had been made of the fact that Mr Henderson's colleagues in the War Cabinet were strongly opposed to British representation at Stockholm, which had been made very clear at the meeting held on August 8". Next morning there was another gathering of the quinquevirs at which it is minuted that they "continued their discussion on the situation created by the Labour Party's vote in favour of representation at the Stockholm Conference".

But new factors had arisen since the previous meeting. One was that Arthur Henderson overnight had tendered his resignation. During the meeting Lloyd George was told "that His Majesty The King had given his permission for the acceptance of Mr Henderson's resignation". *(11.viii.1917)* It was suggested, however, that "it was important particularly in view of Mr Henderson's offer of continued assistance, not to make a wider breach with him than could be avoided". So it was agreed that the Prime Minister should write a letter to Henderson making clear the attitude of the War Cabinet, and that the correspondence should be published in the newspapers. The letter accused Henderson of taking an action which did not appear "to have been fair either to the Government or to the delegates whom you were addressing".

On that same Saturday they went on to discuss further the possible consequences of this row with the Labour Party. Under the rubric "The political situation", the minute ran that:

> "It was generally agreed that the action of the Labour Party was likely to damage this country in the eyes of foreign Powers, who would say that British democracy had by its vote shown itself tired of the war, and that it would also be a serious blow to the Government".

What were they to do? One suggestion was "that a general election should be held immediately, without waiting for the new register, in order that the direct authority of the whole country might be behind the Government in their future conduct of the war". But apart from the fact that women, having no vote, would regard themselves "as being betrayed by the Government" it was pointed out that "when proposals for peace had actually been made by the Pope, and other proposals of a plausible nature but tending towards an unsatisfactory peace were in the air" it was a moment "most inopportune for a general election". So they decided to think it over very carefully and, in the end, no general election was held.

Moreover, the Labour Party decided that one of its representatives should stay in the War Cabinet from which the Leader of the Party had been ejected – or, as far as formalities go, had ejected himself. So the anxieties of the British War Cabinet over

Stockholm were assuaged – but at a cost of the eventual reassertion of Labour's independence in Parliament, the reconstitution of the Labour Party, and its adoption the next year of a broadly socialist basis.

Stockholm, however, was not completely dead. "Many people are taking an interest again in the Stockholm Conference" was the opening sentence of an article by Lenin appearing on September 8, in the paper *Rabochy* No 2.

> "From the outset the revolutionary Social-Democrats, *ie* the Bolsheviks, were against participating in the conference, as a matter of principle. Everyone knows that on the attitude to the war socialists in all countries, belligerent and neutral alike, are split into two large, main divisions. Some took the side of their governments, of their bourgeoisie. These we call social-chauvinists, *ie* socialists in words and chauvinists in action. A chauvinist is one who conceals defence of the predatory interests of 'his own' ruling classes with the concept 'defence of the fatherland'. In the present war, the bourgeoisie of both belligerent coalitions are pursuing predatory aims: the German bourgeoisie are fighting to plunder Belgium, Serbia etc, the British and French bourgeoisie are fighting to plunder the German colonies etc, and the Russian bourgeoisie are fighting to plunder Austria (Lvov) and Turkey (Armenia, Constantinople).
>
> "Hence, those socialists who have come down on the side of their bourgeoisie in the war have ceased to be socialists, have betrayed the working class and have, in effect, deserted to the camp of the bourgeoisie. They have become class enemies of the proletariat."

Lenin's argument continued:

> "Everywhere the workers are showing, in a more or less clear and sharp form, that they realise the social-chauvinists are betraying socialism, that they hate and despise the more prominent social-chauvinists such as Plekhanov in Russia, Scheidemann in Germany, Guesde, Renaudel and Co in France, Hyndman and others in Britain etc, etc.
>
> "A revolutionary internationalist trend has arisen in all countries during the war, despite the gagging and ruthless persecution by the bourgeoisie. This trend has remained loyal to socialism. It has not yielded to chauvinism, has not allowed chauvinism to be covered up by lying phrases about defence of the fatherland. It has exposed the utterly fraudulent nature of these phrases and the absolutely criminal nature of the war, which the bourgeoisie of both coalitions pursue for purposes of plunder. This trend includes, for example, Maclean in Britain, who has been sentenced to eighteen months' hard labour for opposing the predatory British bourgeoisie,

and Karl Liebknecht in Germany ...."

Lenin's argument went on to say that this was the only trend that was loyal to socialism.

"It is the only trend that has not failed the solemn declaration of convictions, the solemn pledge made in November 1912 in the Basle Manifesto which was unanimously signed by the socialists of the world, of every country without exception. The Manifesto speaks not of war in general – there are wars and wars – but of the war which everyone in 1912 clearly saw was being prepared, and which broke out in 1914, the war between Germany and Britain and their allies for world domination. With this war in the offing, the Basle Manifesto does not say a word about the duty or right of socialists to 'defend their fatherland' (ie to justify their participation in the war)."

Lenin concluded his article in a polemic with Maxim Gorky's paper *Novaya Zhizn (New Life)*:

"The would-be internationalists of *Novaya Zhizn* are behaving like intellectual impressionists, *ie* like people who spinelessly yield to the moods of the moment and forget the fundamental principles of internationalism. The *Novaya Zhizn* people reason as follows: since British imperialism is opposed to the Stockholm Conference, we must be for it; it shows that the conference has acquired a significance it has not had so far.

"To reason like that actually means abandoning principles, for German imperialism is at present in favour of the Stockholm Conference because of its own selfish and predatory imperialist interests. What is the value of the 'internationalism' of 'internationalists' who are afraid of openly admitting this indisputable and obvious fact, who have to hide from it? What guarantee have you, gentlemen, that by taking part in the Stockholm Conference together with the Scheidemanns, Staunings and Co you will not virtually become a plaything, a tool in the hands of the secret diplomats of German imperialism? You cannot have any such guarantee. There is none. Even if it does take place, which is very improbable, the Stockholm Conference will be an attempt by the German imperialists to explore the possibilities of such and such an exchange of annexations. That will be the true, the actual significance of the eloquent speeches of the Scheidemanns, Skobelevs and Co." [2]

Notes

1   The War Cabinet really had misjudged Ramsay MacDonald whose standpoint on the parties in Russia as early as May 1917 seems not to have been so remote from their own. At the Leicester May Day Demonstration to welcome the Russian Revolution he spoke of "the Lenin Party, which was composed of thoughtless anarchists, who had no definite policy ...." (*Leicester Post*, Monday, May 7, 1917) It would be difficult to think of a description so little in accordance with the facts.

2   Lenin, *Collected Works*, Vol 25, pp 269-273.

Appendix V

The Russian Scene viewed from the British War Cabinet

WC 229, September 7, 1917

The Situation in Russia

13. The War Cabinet invited General Knox, who was present, to give impressions of the Russian situation.

General Knox referred to his dispatch on Supply and Transport, dated August 10 (*GT*-1917), and said that there were three powerful forces tending to drive the Russians to make a separate peace.

The great mass of the soldiers did not want to fight. They had not wanted to fight before the Revolution, but had been forced on by their officers. There had been frequent cases of indiscipline before the Revolution; and now they were quite general.

In the second place, workmen were making huge economic demands on their employers, and British manufacturers were closing factories and moving away. It was expected that there would shortly be a general lock-out. The workmen had probably enough money to last them for a month; after that time, there would be a state of anarchy. The Government had repeatedly promised to organise a militia or police force in Petrograd and Moscow, but nothing had been done.

The third force was the confusion on the railways. There was an enormous surplus of grain in the Caucasus, but the level at which the price of bread had been fixed was not such as to tempt the peasants to part with their grain. Nor would cash purchases at high prices attract them. They preferred to barter grain for goods which they actually wanted, such as agricultural implements and calico.

Force would have to be applied if the grain was to be forthcoming. The harvest in the Volga governments had been a failure, and to bring the grain from the Northern Caucasus and Western Siberia was very difficult owing to the condition of rolling stock. In June 1916, 18 per cent of the engines were under repair; in June 1917, 24 per cent; and the number was increasing at the rate of 2 per cent per week. The average number of days per month worked in some of the repairing shops was only 13. Thousands of the workmen were constantly attending meetings. The American Railway Mission had not been successful, chiefly because it failed to realise the necessity of taking the initiative in dealing with Orientals. The Russians must be ordered what to do. Just as the scarcity of bread following on the railway crisis had produced the Revolution, so the same forces might lead the people to clamour for a separate peace.

In reply to questions as to the likelihood of a *coup d'état* headed by General Korniloff, General Knox said that he did not know what preparations were being made. When he left Russia, on August 18, Korniloff and Savinkoff were in agreement. Korniloff was a strong character, an honest patriot, and the best man in sight. He had the support of the Cossacks. They numbered 1,000 squadrons of 150 each. He (General Knox) had no faith in Kerenski, and had heard rumours that Kerenski's party had accepted money from Germany. Kerenski was afraid of shedding blood and was allowing matters to drift towards anarchy. A force of 10,000 loyalists would be enough to subdue Petrograd – the main source of disorder – for the Russians were cowards. If Kerenski were to suggest a separate peace he would certainly have the great majority of the country with him. As to some of the prominent generals in Russia, Alexeieff was a student of war and not suited to a crisis; Brusiloff was a politician; Kaledin, the commander of the 8th Army, was one of the best generals and had been chosen by the Cossacks of the Don as their chief. The 12th Army, which was now retreating from Riga, was the worst army.

In concluding his statement, General Knox strongly urged on the War Cabinet the importance of the Allied Governments making a joint representation to the Russian Government recommending that in view of Russia's desperate situation and the peril of putting back democracy, General Korniloff should be fully supported in the measures which he wished to take to restore discipline at the front, on the railways, and in Petrograd.

3 The Socialist Proletarian Revolution

1 From Spring to Autumn 1917

Events moved fast in Russia. The first big change took place at the beginning of May when, as we have seen, the strength of popular feeling compelled both Guchkov and Milyukov to resign. As a result a coalition government was formed of 10 capitalist ministers and 6 ministers drawn from the Socialist Revolutionary and Menshevik parties, which were in the majority in the Soviets.

The new coalition Government not only continued the same foreign policy as its predecessor, but made preparations under the new War Minister Kerensky for a renewed military offensive; during all this time there had been a sort of standstill on the whole front. In addition they began to prepare measures against the Bolsheviks. This, however, was not so easy. For each demonstration called by the Soviet, such as the one on June 18, was turned by the mass of the people (and there were nearly 400,000 in Petrograd on June 28) against the war and against the Provisional Government. It showed that the Bolsheviks were becoming more popular with the masses with every day that passed. Louder and louder sounded their slogans: "Down with the capitalist Ministers! ...", "All Power to the Soviets of Workers', Soldiers' and Peasants' Deputies! ...", "Bread! Peace! Freedom!" In response to the pressure of the Entente powers, exercised directly through their embassies, Alexander Kerensky as Minister of War stimulated the army to fresh military efforts by frenzied orations. On July 1 under General Brusilov the Russian Armies on the South-Western Front made a big drive forward into Galicia and captured thousands of Austrian prisoners. The effect on the Allies, who judged events in Russia solely from the standpoint of winning the war, was reassuring. But inside Russia, where everything was judged from the standpoint of winning the peace, the effect was far otherwise. Signs of a renewed revolt began to show themselves. In mid-July, matters same to a head. The counter-revolution had laid its plans and the following was the sequence of events.

On July 15 the capitalist ministers resigned from the coalition government in order to force the ministers drawn from the majority parties of the Soviets to come to terms as very junior partners with the capitalist parties. But the effect on the masses in Petrograd of this resignation of the 10 capitalist ministers was a series of huge armed demonstrations demanding that the Provisional Government should now depend solely upon the Soviets. The demonstration of July 17 in Petrograd, with over half a million workers and soldiers taking part, was attacked on the orders of the Provisional Government, with the help of Tsarist officers, who fired on the demonstrators, killing over 400 people. While all was at fever heat the Provisional Government arranged for the publication of forged documents purporting to show that Lenin was a German spy and that the Bolshevik agitation was a plot of the German General Staff against the Provisional Government. The forgery was vouched for by Alexinsky, a former associate of Lenin at the beginning of the century, whose degeneration into a provocateur and forger had already been exposed by liberals and socialist Russian exiles in France before the Revolution.

After suppressing the demonstration of workers and soldiers (and the streets of Petrograd ran with their blood) the Mensheviks and SRs in alliance with the capitalists and the White Guard generals fell upon the Bolshevik Party. The *Pravda* premises were wrecked. The *Soldatskaya Pravda (Soldiers' Truth)* and other Bolshevik newspapers were suppressed. For selling *Listok Pravdy (Truth Bulletin)* a worker named Voinov was killed by Cadets in a street in Petrograd. It is now named after him, and regularly decorated with flowers. The revolutionary units of the Petrograd garrison were withdrawn from the capital and sent to the trenches. Widespread arrests were carried out both at the front and at the rear. On July 20 a warrant was issued for Lenin's arrest, and thereafter for another 14 weeks Lenin was being hunted down and sought for. The charge against him, as against a number or other prominent Bolsheviks who were arrested, was to be high treason. The charge was fabricated at the headquarters of General Denikin in the south and based on the testimony of spies and agent provocateurs. At the same time the death penalty, which had been abolished in the first days of the Revolution in mid-March, was restored. The Central Committee of the Party decided that Lenin must go into hiding, from which he was not allowed to emerge, so great was the danger of assassination. The endeavour was to terrorise the vanguard of the working class and drive the Bolsheviks underground.

The next step was the pressure from the capitalists upon the coalition government which was re-formed with Alexander Kerensky as prime minister on terms put forward by the Cadets, namely that the Socialist ministers must be entirely independent of the Soviets.

Meanwhile, in spite of the suppression, the 6th Congress of the Bolshevik Party met in Petrograd. It was 5 years since, in Prague, the Bolsheviks had held their conference, 10 years since the Russian Social-Democratic Labour Party had met in its 5th Congress in London. Now it met secretly for ten days from August 6 to16. Thus, 5 months after the overthrow of Tsardom, the period of freedom was over. The Bolsheviks were compelled to meet in secret, while Lenin, the leader of the working-class party, was forced to go into hiding and to take refuge in a little shanty near Razliv Station. The Congress showed that in the four months since the Revolution on March 12, membership had increased 6-fold from 40,000 to nearly a quarter of a million members.

The government called a 'State conference' from which the Bolshevik Party was excluded. The commander-in-chief Kornilov demanded a declaration by this body in favour of a severe regime. General Kaledin of the Don Cossacks demanded that the Soviets should be abolished and the army should be kept out of politics. It was the public preparation and the speeches which sounded the tocsin for a counter-revolutionary coup d'état. This should have happened at the time of the State conference, August 25-28, but for a one-day protest strike of Moscow workers where the conference was being held. Nearly half a million came out into the streets. The coup d'état the counter-revolutionaries planned had to be postponed.

In Britain the press was quite unable to give a true or understandable picture during that summer and early autumn of the events moving to the highest peak of revolution.

The messages of British correspondents in Petrograd reflect the chaos in government, and also the older institutions, whilst they could make nothing of the new forms of organisation. Relying on statements by the old officials, or by a rapid succession of changing ministers, they had no light to cast. Indeed, usually their Russian sources of information, however oracular, were equally at a loss.

Throughout summer and autumn, right up to the eve of the 'October' Revolution on November 7, their messages were increasingly fragmentary, disjointed and even meaningless. The crisis in the Provisional Government; the creeping reaction and suppression; the rapid emergence of bolder and bolder counter-revolutionary moves and preparations for a *coup d'état* by extreme reaction – these found the British public at large in the dark and wholly unprepared.

In Russia, however, the Bolsheviks had drawn the conclusion that they must prepare for an armed rising against the counter-revolution. For whilst measures were being discussed to restore 'law and order', General Kornilov and his backers – Tsarist generals, Cadets (Constitutional Democrats), the banking and industrial circles – thought there was no need to take two bites of a cherry. Why trouble to establish a military dictatorship behind the facade of a Kerensky Government which would presently have to be dealt with anyhow?

Kerensky, learning on September 8 that Kornilov with regiments of picked troops was marching on Petrograd to proclaim himself dictator, was forced to charge Kornilov with high treason. But it was not he who took action against Kornilov, it was the Bolsheviks. They mobilised the workers and soldiers of Petrograd. They sent trains filled with agitators to meet the advancing troops of Kornilov. By the time Kornilov's troops had got within measurable distance of Petrograd, they themselves had become more than half-revolutionary and quite unsuited to carry out a counter-revolution. The Kornilov attempt was defeated.

For the Russian people it had been an eye-opener. From this moment onwards there was an extremely rapid swing to the side of the Bolsheviks. Once again resounded the slogans: "All Power to the Soviets! ... Bread! Peace! Freedom!" Before the end of September most of the trade unions had a Bolshevik majority in their leading organs. A few weeks later in the elections to the Moscow borough councils the Bolsheviks had 52% of the total vote of all the classes of the population. To these local councils there were elected 350 Bolsheviks, 184 Cadets, 104 SRs,

31 Mensheviks and several non-party. In Moscow the workers and soldiers en masse had gone Bolshevik. The Petrograd Soviet was now being re-elected, and the result was an overwhelming Bolshevik majority.

All this while hunger was growing. Each week of the Provisional Government (now once more transformed into a Directorate led by Kerensky) brought bitter disillusion, bitter enlightenment. In mid-September, as Lenin wrote:

> "During a revolution, millions and tens of millions of people learn in a week more than they do in a year of ordinary, somnolent life. For at the time of a sharp turn in the life of an entire people it becomes particularly clear what aims the various classes of the people are pursuing, what strength they possess, and what methods they use."[1]

A similar process was to be seen amongst the 12 million soldiers; their agonies were being prolonged by the Kerensky Government, instead of being relieved as they had hoped in their longing for peace.

A similar process was also at work in the countryside. There, the vast majority of the population dwelt and worked as peasants. Already they were learning not to put their trust in the earlier-elected leaders of the Soviets. Chernov, as leader of the SRs, had given out slogans for the peasants; Chernov as Minister of Agriculture held back the peasants from carrying out his own slogans. The peasants began to take action on their own and as a reprisal punitive expeditions were sent against them. A break appeared in the ranks of the SRs, the party which up till then had commanded the adherence of the peasantry. The Petrograd conference of the Socialist-Revolutionary Party on September 23, conducted under the leadership of the Left Wing (Spiridonova, Kamkov, Karelin), demanded the end of coalition and the formation of a government based solely on the Soviets.

It was clear that all was becoming ripe for insurrection. By the second week of October, Lenin in his article on the aims of the Revolution stated:

> "The poverty of the poor peasants, the horrors of the war, the horrors of hunger – all these are showing the masses more and more clearly the correctness of the proletarian path, the need to support the proletarian revolution."[2]

Thus in September and throughout October 1917, the vast landslide was in motion – the movement of the peasant and petty-bourgeois masses onto the same path as the town worker and the soldiers of the army.

2 The insurrection

The significance of the vast landslide of the workers, soldiers, peasants, artisans and others was enormous. It meant that the ground was crumbling away beneath the feet of the Provisional Government, now the Directorate, and its backers. All the more desperately the 'dark forces' prepared for a further attempt at counter-revolution. This was evidenced in the fragmentary messages that reached Britain and in the behaviour of those about the embassies.

As this became clear, Lenin all the more earnestly strove to anticipate any such attempt by an immediate transfer of power to the Soviets. He was in hiding in Finland. All through September and October the tone of his letters and articles became more and more urgent. At this particular moment Lenin was expressing through the voice of a single man the agony and the urgent desire of millions of mankind. With Lenin were the majority of the Central Committee of the Bolsheviks. But inside this body there was some resistance, raising of problems and backsliding. Then difficulties were encountered in the Petrograd Soviet. Just before the 6th Congress of the Bolsheviks in August, Trotsky had joined their ranks. He had not been wholeheartedly in the same organisation of the Party with Lenin and the other Bolsheviks for 14 years. In mid-September 1917 Trotsky was elected Chairman of the Petrograd Soviet. There he questioned the timing of the Revolution; with its necessity he was fully agreed, but he insisted strongly on its coincidence with the Second Congress of Soviets which was due to meet on November 7 in the evening. With the utmost urgency Lenin fought against this linking of dates. On the very eve of the insurrection, on November 6, Lenin was compelled to write a *Letter to Central Committee Members* in which he said:

> "In fact it is now absolutely clear that to delay the uprising would be fatal. With all my might I urge comrades to realise that everything now hangs by a thread; that we are confronted by problems which are not to be solved by conferences or congresses (even congresses of Soviets), but exclusively by peoples, by the masses, by the struggle of the armed people.
>
> …
>
> "History will not forgive revolutionaries for procrastinating when they could be victorious today (and they certainly will be victorious today), while they risk losing much tomorrow, in fact, they risk losing everything. If we seize power today, we seize it not in opposition to the Soviets but on their behalf.
>
> "The seizure of power is the business of the uprising; its political purpose will become clear after the seizure.
>
> "It would be a disaster, or a sheer formality, to await the wavering vote of October 25. The people have the right and are in duty bound to decide such questions not by a vote, but by force; in critical moments of revolution, the people have the right and are in duty bound to give directions to their representatives, even their best representatives, and not to wait for them.
>
> "This is proved by the history of all revolutions; and it would be an infinite

crime on the part of the revolutionaries were they to let the chance slip, knowing that the salvation of the revolution, the offer of peace, the salvation of Petrograd, salvation from famine, the transfer of the land to the peasants depend upon them.

"The government is tottering. It must be given the death-blow at all costs.

"To delay action is fatal."[3]

Lenin had arrived that day secretly in the Smolny Institute, by then the headquarters, and had immediately taken charge. As he wrote these words, directions were being given. Already by 5 pm on November 6, revolutionary forces had begun to act. They occupied the Central Telegraph Office and by 9 pm the Petrograd Telegraph Agency. Late that night of November 6, the Red Guard units occupied the four main railway stations, the power plant, the State Bank and other institutions and key points in the capital. By the morning of November 7, the capital was in their hands.[4]

Early in the morning of November 7, detachments of soldiers from the Petrograd District Garrison and Red Guards from the Petrograd factories had occupied all strategic naval and military positions. By mid-day Kerensky and the other ministers, now in the Winter Palace beside the Neva, found that they had been completely surrounded and their motor cars, which had been parked outside, were no longer available for them to make a getaway. Kerensky, however, managed to slip out. Early in the morning Lenin was receiving the final reports. He learned that with hardly any bloodshed the insurrection had been carried through successfully in the capital. He wrote a proclamation as follows and it was issued at 10 am in the name of the Revolutionary Committee of which he had now taken over the leadership.

"To the Citizens of Russia!

"The Provisional Government has been deposed. State power has passed into the hands of the organ of the Petrograd Soviet of Workers' and Soldiers' Deputies – the Revolutionary Military Committee, which heads the Petrograd proletariat and the garrison.

"The cause for which the people have fought, namely, the immediate offer of a democratic peace, the abolition of landed proprietorship, workers' control over production, and the establishment of Soviet power – this cause has been secured.

"Long live the revolution of workers, soldiers and peasants!"[5]

That afternoon at 2.35 a meeting was held of the Petrograd Soviet and Lenin appeared in public – for the first time since July 20 when the manhunt to catch him had been unleashed.[6] The newspaper report of Lenin's statement on this occasion ended with the words:

"The proposal we make to international democracy for a just and immediate peace will everywhere awaken an ardent response among the international proletarian masses. All the secret treaties must be immediately published in order to strengthen the confidence of the proletariat."

After a reference to the peasants he ended by saying:

> "We have now learned to make a concerted effort. The revolution that has just been accomplished is evidence of this. We possess the strength of mass organisation, which will overcome everything and lead the proletariat to the world revolution. We must now set about building a proletarian socialist state in Russia. Long live the world socialist revolution!"[7]

The year 1917 gave him the first chance to speak in public in his native land for over 10 years.

3   Evening of November 7

Meanwhile within the Winter Palace and adjoining buildings, doubly encircled by seven regiments together with Red Guards, the Ministers were refusing to surrender. At last, word was given to storm the Winter Palace. The cruiser *Aurora* which, with three other warships had come up from Kronstadt naval base that morning and was now anchored at the opposite bank of the wide River Neva, was to give the signal. When its big gun thundered out at 9.45 pm it was the signal to attack. In a very short space of time inside the Winter Palace and adjoining buildings the surrender of the inhabitants began. Finally the Ministers, moving about from room to room, were arrested and led to the Peter and Paul Fortress. Those who had been issuing orders to arrest the Military Revolutionary Committee of the Soviet, and to destroy and suppress the Bolshevik newspapers, found themselves (without any casualties) lodged securely in cells for the time being. Tsarist generals captured in arms against the Revolution and put in cells were soon afterwards released on parole.[8]

By ten o'clock in the evening the Second Congress of Soviets was ready to open. There were present some 670 delegates.[9]

At 10.40 pm the Congress was opened by the Menshevik leader Dan on behalf of the Central Executive Committee of the First Congress of Soviets which had been held four months earlier from June 16 to July 7. After the election of a presidium by proportional representation basis, the discussion began. It went on for nearly 7 hours. Then a Proclamation was adopted.

This Proclamation[10] declared that the Second All-Russian Congress had opened and that:

> "Backed by the will of the vast majority of the workers, soldiers and peasants,

backed by the victorious uprising of the workers and the garrison which has taken place in Petrograd, the Congress takes power into its own hands."

Then after intimating that the majority of the members of the Provisional Government were already under arrest it stated that:

> "The Soviet Government will propose an immediate democratic peace to all the nations and an immediate armistice on all fronts."

After stating that all nations inhabiting Russia would have the "genuine right to self-determination" there came a mandatory paragraph:

> "The Congress decrees: all power in the localities shall pass to the Soviets of Workers', Soldiers' and Peasants' Deputies, which must guarantee genuine revolutionary order."

As day was dawning on the capital of old Russia the delegates dispersed. They had decreed the creation of the Soviet State. And the morning and the evening of November 8 were the first day.

The British press was profoundly out of touch. The most sober and accurate of Fleet Street newspapers, the *Manchester Guardian*, at the very time the delegates to the Congress of Soviets were dispersing on the morning after the Revolution, published two messages far from reality – indeed, an epoch behind the day's news.

They dealt with a dispute beginning the previous Sunday between the General Staff of the Military District of Petrograd and the Revolutionary Military Committee of the Soviet, which was trying to strengthen the democratic elements within the staff. This Revolutionary Military Committee of the Petrograd Soviet clearly had felt reason to doubt the revolutionary loyalty of some of the leading officers. The messages ran as follows:

Manchester Guardian, Thursday, November 8, 1917
SOVIET COMMITTEE'S DEMANDS
Petrograd, Tuesday

According to further details concerning the dispute which has arisen between the Revolutionary Military Committee recently created by the Petrograd Soviet and the General Staff of Petrograd military district, the members of the Committee on the night of November 4 called upon the General Staff and demanded the right to control all its orders and to participate in its military deliberations.

Colonel Polkovnikoff (Commander-in-Chief of the troops in the Petrograd district), having refused the demands of the Soviet, the latter at once convened a meeting of the delegates from the garrison, who sent to each regiment a telephone message announcing, as the result of the uncompromising attitude of the General Staff, which refused to recognise the Revolutionary Committee, the Soviet had decided to break off its relations with the General Staff, which would henceforth be considered as an anti-democratic organisation.

At the same time the message invited the troops only to observe orders signed by the Revolutionary Military Committee.

The Revolutionary Committee also addressed to the soldiers and workers and the population of Petrograd a communication stating that it had appointed special commissioners, who were declared to be inviolable, to undertake the military direction of the most important points in Petrograd and surrounding districts.

When the Provisional Government learned of the action of the Revolutionary Committee it ordered that the latter's telephone instructions should be cancelled. The Committee refused to do this, however, and decided to resist the Government.

With this object machine-gun detachments were moved to the headquarters of the Soviet.

In these circumstances, the Government resolved not to have recourse to armed force for the time being, hoping for a peaceful settlement of the dispute.

A plenary sitting of the Government yesterday evening decided to regard the Revolutionary Military Committee as an illegal organisation.   The Minister of Justice was asked to prosecute the members of the Committee, and it was proposed that the military authorities should take all necessary measures in case of revolt against the Government. –*Reuter.*

Manchester Guardian, Thursday, November 8, 1917
DEMAND FOR CONTROL OF MILITARY.
GOVERNOR'S RESISTANCE.
Petrograd, Tuesday, 7 pm

The dispute between the General Staff of the military district of Petrograd and the Revolutionary Military Committee of the Soviet became considerably aggravated last night, when negotiations begun on the basis of strengthening the democratic elements of the Staff were broken off.

The Committee, having been informed that the Military Governor of Petrograd had summoned during the night troops from the environs of the capital, notably from Peterhof, Pavlovsk, and Tsarskoe Selo, ordered these troops not to obey the government.

The situation was also complicated by three Maximalist[11] and two Right party's newspapers being suspended by M Kerensky.

About five o'clock yesterday afternoon the authorities ordered the brigades to be disconnected, and the city is now guarded by troops who are faithful to the Government. –*Reuter*.

The "faithful troops" were, in fact, proving their faith in the Soviets, who that evening of Thursday November 8, began the second session of their historic Congress.

4 Evening of November 8

The first act of the Soviet Congress that evening was to abolish capital punishment in the army which had been restored by Kerensky. Congress then ordered the release of all officers and soldiers in prison for revolutionary activity and all members of land committees arrested by orders of the Kerensky Government, and lastly Kerensky was to be arrested when found. Kerensky had that day published a *prikaz* which he had launched at Pskov when he fled from the capital, in which he had ended by saying:

> "I order all the chiefs and commissars, in the name of the safety of the country, to stay at their posts, and I myself retain the post of Supreme Commander until the Provisional Government of the Republic proclaims its will."

This was published in *Volya Naroda*; but the answer was already given. That day on the walls there was the placard:

FROM THE ALL-RUSSIAN CONGRESS OF SOVIETS

The ex-Ministers Konovalov, Kishkin, Tereshchenko, Maliantovitch, Nikitin and others have been arrested by the Military Revolutionary Committee. Kerensky has fled. All Army organisations are ordered to take every measure for the immediate arrest of Kerensky and his conveyance to Petrograd.

All assistance given to Kerensky will be punished as a serious crime against the State.

Then came the great debate on peace. Lenin had written out a draft *Decree on Peace*. He had not yet attended the Congress held in the Smolny Institute overlooking the River Neva. But now he came onto the platform. Before 1917 he had been in prison, in exile in Siberia or abroad for no less than 17 out of 20 years. For most delegates who had never seen him he was a legendary figure. Eye-witnesses have described the scene. In his *Ten Days that Shook the World* John Reed, American journalist, wrote:

"It was just 8.40 when a thundering wave of cheers announced the entrance of the presidium, with Lenin – great Lenin – among them. A short, stocky figure, with a big head set down in his shoulders, bald and bulging. Little eyes, a snubbish nose, wide, generous mouth, and heavy chin; clean-shaven now, but already beginning to bristle with the well-known beard of his past and future. Dressed in shabby clothes, his trousers much too long for him. Unimpressive, to be the idol of a mob, loved and revered as perhaps few leaders in history have been. A strange popular leader – a leader purely by virtue of intellect; colourless, humourless, uncompromising and detached, without picturesque idiosyncrasies – but with the power of explaining profound ideas in simple terms, of analysing a concrete situation. And combined with shrewdness, the greatest intellectual audacity."

A A Andreyev, who was present as a delegate, recollected:

"When Lenin appeared on the platform, the audience stood up and moved towards him. For a long time he was unable to begin his speech because of round after round of applause and shouts of *Long Live Lenin*. It would be hard to describe the excitement in the hall. The applause was punctuated with cries of jubilation. In addition to the delegates, the hall was packed to capacity with workers, soldiers and sailors who were in Smolny at the time the session opened. People climbed onto window sills, ledges of the columns and chairs just to catch sight of Lenin standing on the platform. Workers, soldiers and sailors kept tossing their hats and caps into the air and raising aloft their rifles."

Lenin waited until the storm of greeting died down, but it was only after his repeated requests that the delegates at last became silent. His speech[12] began with the words: "The question of peace is a burning question, the painful question of the day." Since so much had been said and written and since all the delegates had discussed it he said, "Permit me, therefore, to proceed to read a declaration which the Government you elect should publish." And he began to read his draft *Decree on Peace*. All the belligerent nations and their governments were called upon to start "immediate negotiations for a just and democratic peace", that is, a peace without annexation and without indemnities. To facilitate negotiation it was proposed that the belligerents conclude an armistice for not less than three months to leave time for the completion of negotiations for peace and the summoning of the representative assemblies for the final ratification of the peace terms.

In the course of the decree it was stated that the peace terms, which should be "equally just to all nationalities without exception", were not an ultimatum but that the Soviet would await terms to be stated by other governments. The decree went on:

"The Government abolishes secret diplomacy and for its part announces its firm intention to conduct all negotiations quite openly in view of the whole people. It will proceed immediately with the full publication of the secret treaties endorsed or concluded by the Governments of landowners and capitalists from February up to October 25."

Furthermore the Government proclaimed "The unconditional and immediate annulment" of everything in these secret treaties which secured the advantages and privileges for Russian landowners and capitalists or annexations made by Great Russians. Perhaps the most significant of the terms of the decree was the last paragraph in which it was said that, while this proposal for peace was addressed to the governments and peoples of all the belligerent countries, the Government of Russia

"appeals in particular also to the class-conscious workers of the three most advanced nations of mankind and the largest states participating in the present war, namely, Great Britain, France, and Germany. The workers of these countries have made the greatest contributions to the cause of progress and socialism; they have furnished the great examples of the Chartist movement in England, a number of revolutions of historic importance effected by the French proletariat, and, finally, the heroic struggle against the Anti-Socialist Law in Germany …."

Then the spirit of the Basle resolution which he himself had helped to draft 10 years earlier was recalled when the final words of the *Decree on Peace* rang out:

"All these examples of proletarian heroism and historical creative work are a pledge that the workers of the countries mentioned will understand the duty that now faces them of saving mankind from the horrors of war and its consequences, that these workers, by comprehensive, determined, and supremely vigorous action, will help us to conclude peace successfully, and at the same time emancipate the labouring and exploited masses of our population from all forms of slavery and all forms of exploitation."

The reading of the decree of peace was greeted with enthusiasm and one after another the speakers spoke in its support. It was 10.35 when Chairman Kamenev asked for all those in favour of the *Decree on Peace* to hold up their hands. It was greeted with the greatest enthusiasm and adopted with unanimity. Twenty-five years later a history of the Civil War, edited by a board at the head of which stood the name Maxim Gorky, wrote those words:

"At dawn on the day after the Revolution the radio broadcast to the world the great wise words of the Soviet *Decree on Peace*, snapping the iron fetters of the imperialist war. People wept with joy on hearing them, and eyes, long dimmed by despair, shone again with reborn hope."[13]

Next was the decree which confiscated the landlords' land and handed it over to the tillers of the soil.[14] First was the proposal that the landed estates were abolished forthwith without compensation. Landed estates and also all crown, monasterial and church lands, with all their livestock, implements, farm buildings etc, were to be handed over and put at the disposal of the land committees and local Soviets of Peasants' Deputies. It was made a felony to damage the confiscated property, which henceforth belonged to the whole people. Details were given as to how this decree was to be carried out. Amongst these was the statement that land tenure would be on the basis of equality and that there shall be "absolutely no restriction on the forms of land tenure". These forms, whether household, homestead, communal or co-operative, were to be decided in each individual village or settlement. Lastly the decree said: "The land of ordinary peasants and ordinary Cossacks shall not be confiscated." The decree on land was passed with one vote against and 8 abstentions.

Then came the question of the form of government as the last item on the agenda of the Congress. This decree[15] announced that the right to appoint and dismiss People's Commissars would be vested in the All-Russia Congress of Soviets of Workers', Peasants' and Soldiers' Deputies and its Central Executive Committee.

The list of the Council of People's Commissars ran as follows:

Chairman of the Council	Vladimir Ulyanov (Lenin)
People's Commissar of the Interior	A I Rykov
Agriculture	V P Milyutin
Labour	A G Shlyapnikov
Army and Navy Affairs	a committee consisting of: V A Ovseyenko (Antonov), V Krylenko and P Y Dybenko
Commerce and Industry	V P Nogin
Education	A V Lunacharsky
Finance	I I Skvortsov-Stepanov
Foreign Affairs	L D Bronstein (Trotsky)
Justice	G I Oppokov (Lonov)
Food	I A Teodorovich
Posts and Telegraph	N P Avilov (Glebov)
Chairman for the Council on Nationalities	J V Jugashvili (Stalin)

The office of People's Commissar of Railways was temporarily left vacant.

The All-Russia Central Executive Committee of 101 members was composed as follows:

Bolsheviks	62
Left Socialist-Revolutionaries	29
United Internationalist Social Democrats	6
Ukrainian Socialists	3
Socialist Revolutionary of the Maximalist Faction	1

The Congress closed having created the most democratic of all constitutions in the shape of the Soviet State.

These two days of the October Revolution (so-called because they fell upon October 25 and 26 under the old-style calendar[16]) may be said to have marked the beginning of a new civilisation. It was 8 months since the abdication of the Tsar, 4 months since the brief period of freedom in Russia had ended and given place to counter-revolutionary attacks and arrests and manhunts. Now the new epoch was to begin.

5 The impact on the British press

Such in brief was the October Revolution: the insurrection and the taking of power by the Second Congress of Soviets, handed over by the Military Revolutionary Committee of the Petrograd Soviet; the transformation of state power throughout Russia; the setting up of the new government, the Council of People's Commissars. This, however, was not how the news came to London or how it appeared in Fleet Street and the provincial newspapers of the United Kingdom.

Skilled journalists had been anxious, many of them, to learn the truth behind the oracles, the occasional ministerial utterances or army communiqués. But they could not hear it issuing from the larynx of a Kerensky or a Stankevitch.[17] They had been bewildered by each turn of events. Consequently now the messages of the individual correspondents and even those of the sober writers and agencies were examples of men clutching at phantasmal hopes engendered by the wishful thinking of the troubled and embarrassed phantoms of the self-entitled ministers. Messages from Petrograd after November were fragmentary, heavily loaded and in the main despairing.

The official reports of the Embassy, of the Foreign Office, the outpourings of the journalists to their editors, give a measure of their profound bewilderment, intensifed by their hatred of the working people.

The first inkling of the actual insurrections was given in a Wednesday noon 'flash' from Petrograd that "an armed naval detachment, acting under the orders of the Maximalist Revolutionary Committee, has occupied the offices of the official

Petrograd Telegraph Agency". This was followed at 4.25 pm by a further message that:

"The Maximalists have also occupied the Central Telegraph Office, the State Bank and the Marie Palace, where the Preliminary Parliament, the proceedings of which have been suspended in view of the situation, has been holding its sittings. Up to the present no disorders have been reported, with the exception of some outrages by apaches. Street traffic and the general life of the city remains normal."

This was printed on Thursday November 8 under the headlines "Maximalist Rising: Parliament Building Seized".

Manchester Guardian, Friday November 9, 1917
MAXIMALIST COUP.
FORCIBLE SEIZURE OF POWER,
IMMEDIATE PEACE PLAN.
(Admiralty, per Wireless Press)

Thursday

A proclamation, radiated through the wireless stations of the Russian Government today, states that the garrison and proletariat of Petrograd have deposed the Kerensky Government.

ANNOUNCEMENTS BY THE NEW GOVERNMENT.
ARMISTICE TO BE PROPOSED.

Reuter's Agency has received the following telegram from the official Petrograd telegraph agency, which, as was reported last night by Reuter's own correspondent at Petrograd, was occupied in the course of Wednesday by an armed naval detachment acting under the orders of the Maximalist Revolutionary Committee:

November 7, 9.50 pm

The day has brought certain changes in the general situation. In the capital the Maximalist movement has made fresh and fairly appreciable progress, but no disorders have taken place.

Towards five o'clock in the afternoon the Military Revolutionary Committee of the Soviet published a proclamation stating that Petrograd is in its hands, thanks to the assistance of the garrison, which enabled a coup d'etat to be brought about without bloodshed. The proclamation declares that the new

Government will propose an immediate and just peace, will hand the land to the peasants, and will summon a Constituent Assembly.

Manchester Guardian, Friday November 9, 1917
COSSACKS WITH THE SOVIET
November 8, 1.10 am

Delegates of three Cossack regiments quartered here yesterday declared they would not obey the Provisional Government, and would not march against the Council of Workmen's and Soldiers' Delegates, but that they were prepared to maintain public order.

The Petrograd Council of Workmen's and Soldiers' Delegates held an extraordinary meeting in the afternoon, in the course of which the President, M Trotsky, declared that the Provisional Government no longer existed, and that some of the Ministers had been arrested. The Preliminary Parliament, he added, had been dissolved.

M Lenin, who was received with prolonged cheers, made a speech in which he outlined the three problems now before the Russian democracy – first, the immediate conclusion of war for which purpose the new Government must propose an armistice to the belligerents; second, to hand over the land to the peasants; third, the settlement of the economic crisis.

The Assembly then adopted a resolution expressing the wish that these problems should be solved as quickly as possible.

At the close of the sitting a declaration was read from a representative of the Social-Democratic Minimalist party of the Soviet stating that the party disapproved of the coup d'etat and withdrew from the Petrograd Soviet.

Manchester Guardian, Friday November 9, 1917
MINISTERS ARRESTED.
FLIGHT OF M KERENSKY.

Petrograd, Thursday, 11.15 am

The Petrograd official agency transmits the following:

The Congress of Councils of Workmen's and Soldiers' Delegates of All Russia, which opened last evening, this morning issued the following three proclamations:

1. To all the Provincial Councils of Workmen's and Soldiers' and Peasants' Delegates.

All power appertains to the Soviets. The Government commissaries are relieved of their functions. The Presidents of the Soviets are to communicate direct with the Revolutionary Government. All members of the Agricultural Committees who have been arrested are to be set at liberty immediately, and the commissaries who arrested them are to be arrested in their turn.

2. The death penalty re-established by Kerensky at the front is abolished. Complete freedom of political propaganda is re-established at the front. All revolutionary soldiers and officers who have been arrested for complicity in so-called political crimes are to be set at liberty immediately.

3. The ex-Ministers Konovalov, Kischkin, Tereshchenko, Malantovitch, Nikitin and others are arrested by the Revolutionary Committee.

Kerensky has taken to flight. All military bodies are enjoined to take all possible measures to arrest Kerensky and bring him back to Petrograd. All complicity with Kerensky will be dealt with as high treason.

Manchester Guardian, Friday November 9, 1917
THE NEW PROGRAMME.
ORDERS OF THE REVOLUTION COMMITTEE.

According to news transmitted through the wireless stations of the Russian Government the following proclamation has been issued:

To the Army Committees of the active army and to all the Soviets of the Soldiers' Deputies:

The Garrison and proletariat of Petrograd have deposed the Government of Kerensky, which rose against the Revolution and the people.

The change which resulted in the deposition of the Provisional Government was accomplished without bloodshed.

The Petrograd Soviet of the Workmen's and Soldiers' Delegates solemnly welcomes the accomplished change, and proclaims the authority of the Military Revolutionary Committee until the creation of a Government of Soviets.

In announcing this to the army at the front, the Revolutionary Committee calls upon the Revolutionary soldiers to watch closely the conduct of the men in command.

Officers who do not join the accomplished Revolution immediately and openly must be arrested at once as enemies.

The Petrograd Soviet considers as the programme of the new authority:

1. The offer of an immediate democratic peace.
2. Proprietorial lands to the peasants.
3. The transmission of all authority to the Soviets.
4. An honest convocation of the Constitutional Assembly.

The National Revolutionary Army must not permit uncertain military detachments to leave the front for Petrograd.

Use persuasion, but where this fails, oppose any such action on the part of these detachments by force without mercy.

The actual order must be read immediately to all military detachments of all arms. The suppression of this order from the rank and file by the army organisations is equivalent to a great crime against the Revolution, and will be punished by all the strength of the Revolutionary law.

Soldiers! For peace, for bread, for land, for the power of the law and people!

(Signed)

THE MILITARY REVOLUTIONARY COMMITTEE

6 Impact on ruling circles

The fall of the Provisional Government on November 7, 1917 was unexpected in only a limited sense. As far as the ruling circles were concerned they had many weeks before this written off the Russian Revolution as the frustration of their hopes. Once their prime favourite, Kornilov, had been defeated in a manner which enormously strengthened the forces of the real Revolution and brought the Bolsheviks once more to the foreground, there was little hope and expectancy left except that something dreadful might happen. This of course did not apply to the reading public who had been fed on hopeful statements throughout most of the press. But the reality when it came was regarded as something worse than the worst that could have been expected.

News of the Bolshevik Revolution was received in a manner exactly opposite to that in which its first stage had been greeted less than 8 months before. Then there had been universal approbation of something which would help Britain win the war. Now there was almost as universal reprobation. No language strong enough could be found to condemn the Bolsheviks and by implication the workers and peasants of Russia for what they had done. They had upset the castle of cards. They had destroyed illusions. They had brought not only the capitalists and landlords of Russia face to face with stark reality; but they had brought it in a most prominent and unmistakable fashion right beneath the noses of every ruling class in the world. The effect was mingled with feelings of alarm, horror, despondency. It was so bad that many could not believe it. The working class of the capital city of the chief ally of the British Empire had risen in insurrection, disposed of the Government within a few hours and that with scarcely any bloodshed (less actually than had occurred in the month of March 1917). They had combined the power of workers and of the armed forces. The sailors on the four-funnelled cruiser *Aurora* had fired that single shot from the Northern bank of the River Neva which smote with a terrific clangour the ears of ministers in the Winter Palace – and in point of fact has been echoing around the world ever since.

The working class was in control: this it was that caused shudders of horror in every government.

Next following on the insurrection was the news that the Second Congress of Soviets had taken over the reins of government and had proclaimed immediate decrees for bringing peace to all the peoples of the world, land to the numberless peasants of Russia and the promise of bread to relieve the hunger that was threatening the whole country. The *Decree on Peace* was something that cut through all the complicated endeavours of Left-wing Liberals and Socialist leaders everywhere to formulate aims which would eventually make possible a negotiated peace. This was to bring peace immediately.

At first disbelief was very strong. It was considered impossible for the Bolsheviks to remain in power. It is true Lenin had said at a conference in the early summer that there was one party prepared to take power; but everybody had laughed that off. Now that it had happened it was clear that it could not last. First, it was assumed that the forces (largely imaginary) of the true sons and daughters of Russia everywhere, outside the garrisons of the capital and the other towns, would immediately suppress this monstrous insurrection. Secondly, it was believed that the peasantry would be opposed and that this would put paid to the Bolsheviks. In point of fact the Congress of Soviets of Peasants soon did meet and was won over by the powerful arguments of Lenin stating the facts as it affected them and their desire for land and for peace. Thirdly, trust was put in all the other Socialists who had been in a majority in the March elections.

Lastly there was Alexander Kerensky who had come to the fore as the voice of the God of War, the war of the Entente against the Central Empires and who would not tolerate for a moment the continuance of this attempt at government by the working class, peasants and soldiers. Had they not read in their newspapers on Thursday November 8 a Reuter despatch which was reassuring? It told how Alexander Kerensky, speaking on Monday November 5 to the Pre-Parliament, had announced that he would deal severely with all whose efforts were "treason to the Fatherland".

"Government Firm: Kerensky's Declaration in Parliament" had been the headline above the Reuter message sent from Petrograd on Tuesday November 6. Kerensky had said:

> "These efforts are made from two sides – namely, by the extreme Left and Right – urged on by articles by the criminal Lenin, who is a fugitive from justice."

The message continued:

> Turning next to the conflict between the General Staff of the Military Governor

of Petrograd and the Revolutionary Military Committee of the Soviet, M Kerensky said the military power could not recognise as legal the demands made by the committee, and demanded that its orders should be revoked. The committee had made a pretence of entering upon pourparlers, and even displayed a conciliatory tendency, but at the same time it began the clandestine distribution of arms and cartridges to workmen.

"This," he added, "is why I consider that part of the population of Petrograd is in a state of revolt, and I have ordered the immediate opening of an enquiry and the necessary arrests to be made."

The Left here interrupted M Kerensky with ironical shouts, but the Premier, turning towards them, exclaimed: "The Government will be killed rather than cease to defend the honour, security, and independence of the State." M Kerensky then referred to the attitude of the front towards the action of the Maximalists, and read telegrams in which the army demanded energetic measures against excesses in Petrograd, and promised the Government its vigorous support –*Reuter*. (*Manchester Guardian*, Thursday November 8, 1917)

Surely Kerensky was not without resources. Surely there was some hope in this 'heroic' figure.

Yes, it was true. Kerensky had ordered wholesale suppression of Socialist papers, or working-class papers, and this is the counter-revolutionary action of Kerensky preceding the successful Revolution. True, after November 7 and 8, Kerensky had sought to hurl cavalry and infantry, trusted regiments, upon the people of Petrograd. But this attempt, though featured largely in the British press, had collapsed. The cavalry had melted away. The first attempt at counter-revolution after November 7 had failed.

There was, however, the immediate hope that the former Chief of Staff General Alexeyev, together with other generals, could gather forces down in the South. General Kaledin was there; and others were mentioned as being the sure hope of counter-revolution to take the place of Kornilov who had proved such a disappointment.

Furthermore, the liberated nationalities would put paid to the Bolsheviks. The Bolsheviks themselves had proclaimed in the spring conference the right of self-determination of all nationalities; and would now be 'hoist with their own petard'. Since for all these reasons the Proletarian Socialist Revolution was bound to be a flash in the pan or, as Stankevitch announced, "would last only a few hours", there could be no question of recognising this "new government".

Again it was the opposite to what happened in March 1917. Then with astonishing haste the embassies of the Entente had hurried to greet the Provisional Government. Now they would have nothing to do with what was happening either in the Taurida Palace or in the Smolny Institute which these miscreants of Bolsheviks had made into their fortress. The ambassadors did not touch the new government; the foreign offices of the Entente would not touch the new government; it was to be frozen out of existence, this low-caste pseudo-government of the *canaille*, the Untouchables.

They had set the whole capitalist world against them, whether belligerents or neutrals; they had made a revolutionary call to all to stop fighting; they had threatened to publish the Secret Treaties; and there was no-one to stop them doing it.

Notes and References

1   Lenin, *Lessons of the Revolution*, in *Collected Works*, Vol 25, p 229 –*Ed.*
2   Lenin, *The Tasks of the Revolution*, in *Collected Works*, Vol 26, p 59 –*Ed.*
3   Lenin, *Letter to Central Committee Members*, in *Collected Works*, Vol 26, pp 234-5 –*Ed.*
4   It had been October 23 that the Central Committee had decided on insurrection and had had the decision confirmed at an extended Central Committee on October 29. To carry through the insurrection the Central Committee appointed Dubnov, Dzerzhinsky, Stalin, Sverdlov and Uritsky to reinforce the Revolutionary Military Committee appointed a fortnight earlier by the Petrograd Soviet. To these comrades was confided supreme operative direction of the rising. As we have seen the details were carried through by the Revolutionary Military Committee of the Petrograd Soviet. And Lenin, arriving on November 6, had himself taken full charge of all operations.
5   Lenin, *Collected Works*, Vol 26, p 236 –*Ed.*
6   Four days later in the *Manchester Guardian* of Saturday November 11 there appeared a message sent from Petrograd two days earlier at 12.45 pm and headlined "Lenin and his Lieutenant". It described the scene in the Smolny Institute in the following words: "M Lenin, on making his appearance there, received an enthusiastic ovation. He was accompanied by his Lieutenant, M Zinoviev, who was wanted by the late Provisional Government – both of them were unrecognisable – M Lenin had shaved off his moustache while M Zinoviev had grown a beard. *(Reuter)*"
7   Lenin, *Report on the Tasks of Soviet Power*, in *Collected Works*, Vol 26, pp 239-240 –*Ed.*
8   The parole was promptly broken in the case of generals like Krasnov and Dutov who did not believe in keeping faith to the '*canaille*' for they did not regard it as a matter of honour to keep their word given to the lower classes.
9   Composition of Second Congress of Soviets

Soviets of Workers' and Soldiers' Deputies	195
Soviets of Workers', Soldiers' and Peasants' Deputies	104
Soviets of Workers' Deputies	46
Soviets of Soldiers' Deputies	21
Soviets of Peasants' Deputies	19
Soviets of Workers' and Peasants' Deputies	6
Party Representation at the Congress	
Bolshevik Faction	390
Menshevik Faction	72
Left Socialist-Revolutionaries	179
Right and Centre Socialist-Revolutionaries	24

One third of the total number of delegates were from non-Russian parts of the Empire such as the Caucasus, Central Asia and the Baltic Provinces.
10   Lenin, *To Workers, Soldiers and Peasants*, in *Collected Works*, Vol 26, pp 247-8 –*Ed.*
11   Here we have a flagrant instance of the peculiarity of the Fleet Street newspapers in that they would not accept the usual Russian descriptive terms for each body but fastened on the magic word "Maximalist". This caused confusion at the time and for weeks afterwards in the minds of British readers. The journalists did not deign to explain exactly what they meant by "Maximalist", partly because they were themselves in ignorance. It would seem that someone in some press agency had got to know that "Bolshevik" means "men

of the majority", and so decided that these were the "maximum" faction, or "Maximalists".

The Call stated that the Bolsheviks ("so-called Maximalists – that is, followers of Lenin") had been victorious. This explanation sufficed to cover events obviously carried through by the Bolsheviki; but left open how it came about that the Bolsheviki, who were not Maximalists, had stuck on to them by the British press this name which was that of a small group of peasants, an earlier left offshoot of the SRs.

12   Lenin, *Report on Peace*, October 26 (November 8), in *Collected Works*, Vol 26, p 249ff *–Ed.*

13   *History of the Civil War in the USSR, Vol 1: The Prelude to the Great Proletarian Revolution From the beginning of the War to the beginning of October 1917*, J Stalin, M Gorky, S Kirov, V Voroshilov and A Zhdanov, eds, Lawrence & Wishart, 1937 *–Ed.*

14   Lenin, *Report on Land*, in *Collected Works*, Vol 26, p 257ff *–Ed.*

15   Lenin, *Decision to Form the Workers' and Peasants' Government*, in *Collected Works*, Vol 26, pp 262-3 *–Ed.*

16   It was brought up to date three months later at the beginning of February 1918.

17   Even the sober *Manchester Guardian* swallowed (and regurgitated) wild rumours and wilder claims. In its issue of Monday November 12 the headlines ran: "Street fighting in Petrograd – Kerensky returning – Extremist defeats (Admiralty per wireless)" and beneath was quoted a communiqué:

"The liquidation of the Bolshevik adventure is only a matter of days or even hours." The communiqué was issued by the Menshevik V B Stankevitch, who was the Supreme Commissar of General Headquarters.

Appendix

The Proclamation of the Congress of Soviets to Workers, Soldiers and Peasants!

The Second All-Russia Congress of Soviets of Workers and Soldiers' Deputies has opened. The vast majority of the Soviets are represented at the Congress. A number of delegates from the Peasants' Soviets are also present. The mandate of the compromising Central Executive Committee has terminated. Backed by the will of the vast majority of the workers, soldiers and peasants, backed by the victorious uprising of the workers and the garrison which has taken place in Petrograd, the Congress takes power into its own hands.

The Provisional Government has been overthrown. The majority of the members of the Provisional Government have already been arrested.

The Soviet government will propose an immediate democratic peace to all the nations and an immediate armistice on all fronts. It will secure the transfer of the land of the landed proprietors, the crown and the monasteries to the peasant committees without compensation; it will protect the rights of the soldiers by introducing complete democracy in the army; it will establish workers' control over production; it will ensure the convocation of the Constituent Assembly at the time appointed; it will see to it that bread is supplied to the cities and prime necessities to the villages; it will guarantee all the nations inhabiting Russia the genuine right to self-determination.

The Congress decrees: all power in the localities shall pass to the Soviets of Workers', Soldiers' and Peasants' Deputies, which must guarantee genuine revolutionary order.

The Congress calls upon the soldiers in the trenches to be vigilant and firm. The Congress of Soviets is convinced that the revolutionary army will be able to defend the revolution against all attack of imperialism until such time as the new government succeeds in concluding a democratic peace, which it will propose directly to all peoples. The new government will do everything to fully supply the revolutionary army, by means of a determined policy of requisitions and taxation of the propertied classes, and also will improve the condition of the soldiers' families.

The Kornilov men – Kerensky, Kaledin and others – are attempting to bring troops against Petrograd. Several detachments, whom Kerensky had moved by deceiving them, have come over to the side of the insurgent people.

Soldiers, actively resist Kerensky the Kornilovite! Be on your guard!

Railwaymen, hold up all troop trains dispatched by Kerensky against Petrograd!

Soldiers, workers in factory and office, the fate of the revolution and the fate of the democratic peace is in your hands!

Long live the revolution!

The All-Russia Congress of Soviets of Workers' and Soldiers' Deputies
The Delegates from the Peasants' Soviets

Written on October 25 (November 7), 1917
Published in the newspaper *Rabochy i Soldat,* No 9, October 26 (November 8),
1917
(Lenin, *Collected Works,* Vol 26, pp 247-8 –*Ed.*)

4 The Making of Peace

I **The call for a truce**

The mid-November days passed by while the upper and middle classes of Britain heard the news from Russia with an increasing anxiety that was tempered all the while by the stout hope (the strong conviction in the case of the newspaper writers and their millionaire proprietors) that the Socialist Proletarian Revolution would soon collapse. It was about this time that the writings of the neurologist Sigmund Freud were beginning to spread from medical circles into the consciousness of the intellectual pace-setters; and while most journalists were as yet innocent of any Freudian categories, nevertheless the phrases 'wish-fulfilment' and 'wishful thinking' could aptly be applied to the columns of reports, rumours, special articles and pontifical editorials. As late as two months after the victory of the Revolution the leading article in the *Daily Telegraph* could say that the Soviet Government "may be swept out of existence at any hour and no sane man would give them as much as a month to live." *(5.i.1918)*

Each week, as it passed away without the much-expected and longed-for collapse of the Revolution, left behind it a legacy of increasing hostility towards the Soviets of Workers' and Soldiers' Deputies. Wave after wave of class hatred swept through the ranks of the established order in Britain, and was to mount into a flood of frenzied detestation of everything 'Bolshevik'. It was not the Germans, Austrians and Turks but the Bolsheviks who were the most dangerous enemy, in that they 'had forsaken their friends and were puppets of German militarism'. The mounting hysteria of hatred was frequently concentrated against the person of Lenin, as it had been within Russia in the 6 months before October, and was to be until the arch-opponent Churchill in his articles of autumn 1920 was to write of Lenin as "the monster, crawling down from his pyramid of skulls".[1]

Meantime, however, in November 1917, and before the hopes of speedy Bolshevik failure could possibly begin to wane, the horrific news was picked up from the Russian wireless that the *Decree on Peace*, so far from being a mere propagandist declaration, was being put into effect by instructions to the Commander-in-Chief to open up pourparlers for a truce.

This carrying out of the *Decree on Peace*, the formal proposal by the Council of People's Commissaries[2] for an armistice "to all the nations involved in the war, to the Allies and also to the nations at war with us" may have come as an affront to British and French officialdom which for two thirds of a year had refused an Allied discussion on war aims. But, in direct contrast, to those who were longing for peace a door of hope was opened; and, for the small remnant in Britain and France who had maintained the standpoint of international socialism, this call from revolutionary socialists for a general truce on all fronts seemed the guerdon of hope confirmed.

At that same moment the Russian Revolution had the immediate impact of an irreversible action. Throughout the world the name of Lenin sounded as a harbinger of better times, an embodiment of the aspirations of all mankind to have done with the horrors of war and the accumulated evils that imperialism had brought to all lands, whether feudal or capitalist. Already the persecuted in Britain had learned the great name in the summer of 1917: among the war-resisters transferred from the strict seclusion of a "silence rule" goal to a "House of Correction", where the inmates under a more relaxed regime were allowed to decorate their cells, there was one in the last days of August 1917 who observed that the cell opposite to his own had already been inscribed with a garland around the name *Leniniana*. The 'flowery dell' of a prison was flying a signal of hope to all the war resisters there immured.

The Acting Commander-in-Chief, General Dukhonin, did not reply to the message from the Council of People's Commissaries sent to him on November 20 and received at Field Headquarters early the next morning. Thereupon the Soviet Government, having received no reply after 24 hours, empowered three of its members to open up direct-line conversations with Field Headquarters, to find out the cause of this delay. General Dukhonin, wakened up in the early hours of Thursday, November 22 by Lenin, Stalin and Krylenko at the other end of the line, returned at first equivocal answers. Then, given an imperative order in the name of the Soviet Government to open up negotiations for a truce, Dukhonin refused to obey. Thereupon the Soviet Government dismissed him from his post and appointed the War Commissary in his place as Commander-in-Chief.

Wireless messages giving the details were signed by Lenin, and their contents appeared in the British press on the next day as follows:

Manchester Guardian, Friday November 23, 1917
RUSSIAN ARMISTICE OFFER.
COMMANDER-IN-CHIEF DISOBEYS.
ENSIGN SET IN HIS PLACE.
    The following Maximalist order is transmitted through the wireless stations of the Russian Government:
    To all committees of regiments, divisions, corps, armies; to all the soldiers of the revolutionary army; and to all the sailors of the revolutionary navy.
    During the night of November 20 the Council of the People's Commissaries sent a wireless message to the Commander-in-Chief Dukhonin, containing the order that he should immediately and formally offer an armistice to all the nations, allied and hostile, involved in the war.
    This message was received at Headquarters on November 21 at 5.05 am. Dukhonin was instructed to keep the Council of the People's Commissaries continually informed upon the progress of pourparlers, and only to sign the agreement for armistice after sanction by the Council of People's Commissaries.

At the same time a similar offer for an armistice was formally submitted to all the plenipotentiary representatives of the Allies in Petrograd.

Having received no answer from Dukhonin up to yesterday evening, the Council of the People's Commissaries gave the authority to Lenin, Stalin, and Krylenko to ask Dukhonin by direct wire for the cause of such a delay.

The pourparlers have been in progress since 4.30 am today.

Dukhonin has attempted many times to evade giving an explanation of his conduct and a clear answer to the orders of the Government. When a categorical order was sent to Dukhonin instructing him to offer immediately and formally an armistice with the purpose of commencing peace pourparlers he refused to obey.

DUKHONIN DEPOSED.

Now in the name of the Government of the Russian Republic, and by the order of the Council of the People's Commissaries, Dukhonin has been informed that he has been deposed from his functions for disobeying the instructions of the Government, and for conduct which is bringing unheard-of and terrible sufferings to all the working masses, to all the country, and especially to the armies.

At the same time Dukhonin has been ordered to continue his duties till a new Commander-in-Chief or any other person authorised by him arrives to take over the command.

Ensign Krylenko has been appointed the new Commander-in-Chief.

Soldiers, the question of peace is in your hands. You must not permit the counter-revolutionary generals to destroy the great work of peace. You must arrest and guard them well, so that lynch-law, which is not worthy of a revolutionary army, cannot take place, and so that these generals cannot evade imminent justice. You will observe the strongest revolutionary and military discipline.

Let the regiments which are on the frontal positions elect immediately plenipotentiaries who shall formally begin the peace pourparlers with the enemy.

The Council of the People's Commissaries gives you authority for it. On the progress of the pourparlers you shall inform us by all possible means.

Only the Council of the People's Commissaries has the right to sign the final agreement of armistice.

Soldiers, the question of peace is in your hands. Have watchfulness, tenacity, energy, and the will for peace will win.

In the name of the Government of the Russian Republic.

(Signed)   WOULIANOFF-LENIN,
President of the Council of the People's Commissaries
N KRYLENKO

People's Commissary of War, Highest Commander-in-Chief
Petrograd, November 22, 1917

The news was also published from Petrograd that demobilisation was to begin.

Manchester Guardian, Saturday, November 24, 1917
REDUCTION OF THE ARMIES.
DISBANDMENT ORDERED TO BEGIN.
According to Admiralty news issued through the Wireless Press, the following announcement has been issued by the authorities in Petrograd:
Decree: The Workmen's and Peasants' Government of the People's Commissaries has decided to undertake without delay the reduction of the armies and orders to begin with the release from their military duties of all citizen soldiers of the class conscripted in 1899.

The instructions concerning the liberation of other classes from military service will be issued at a later date.

Upon demobilisation all arms must be handed over to regimental committees, which will be responsible for their safety. The Highest Commander-in-Chief is obliged to bring this decree directly to the knowledge of the rank and file.

(Signed)
WOULIANOFF-LENIN, President of the Council of the People's Commissaries
W A OVSKEYENKO-ANTONOFF, N KRYLENKO, People's Commissaries for the War

On the same day came the explanatory official Note to the foreign embassies, of which the *Manchester Guardian* printed the text of the Note to the French, as quoted by Reuter.

Manchester Guardian, Saturday November 24, 1917
NOTE TO THE EMBASSIES.
Petrograd, Thursday.
The Petrograd News Agency announced that the following Note has been sent to the foreign Embassies at Petrograd:
M l'Ambassadeur,
l have the honour to announce that the Congress of Councils of Workmen's, Soldiers' and Peasants' Delegates of All the Russias, instituted on November 8 a new Government of the Republic of All the Russias.

Having been appointed Commissary of Foreign Affairs in this Government, l beg to call to the attention of your Excellency the following words, which have been approved by the Congress of the Delegates of the Councils, and contain proposals for a truce and for a democratic peace without annexation and without indemnities, based on the principle of the independence of nations and of their right to determine the nature of their own development themselves.

I have the honour to suggest that you should consider this document in the light of an official proposal for an immediate truce upon all the fronts, and to take immediate steps to set on foot negotiations for peace. The Government, in the name of the Republic of All the Russias, is addressing the same proposal to all the nations and their Governments.

Pray accept the assurance of the most perfect respect on the part of the Government of the Councils towards the people of France, which still keeps aloof from peace aspirations, as well as to all the other nations who are drained of their blood and exhausted by the prolonged carnage.

(Signed)

L TROTSKY
Petrograd, November 22 *(Reuter)*.

The following day, Friday November 23, *Izvestia* and *Pravda* published the Secret Treaties.

That evening, Lord Robert Cecil made a statement to Reuter's correspondent which the *Manchester Guardian* published on Saturday November 24 as follows:

BOLSHEVIKS "OUTSIDE THE PALE".
LORD R CECIL AND THE QUESTION OF A SEPARATE RUSSIAN PEACE.
LUDENDORFF GONE TO THE EAST FRONT.

The Maximalist Foreign Minister or Commissary for Foreign Affairs, M Trotsky, has addressed a Note to the foreign embassies in Petrograd proposing an immediate truce on all fronts and the opening of negotiations for peace.

Lord Robert Cecil, Minister of Blockade and Under-Secretary for Foreign Affairs, stated last night that if the Russian Extremists made a separate peace it would place them outside the pale of the ordinary Councils of Europe. There would be no question of recognising such a Government.

In connection with the Russian offer of truce General Ludendorff, the German Quartermaster General, is reported to have left for the eastern front with a numerous staff.

RUSSIAN EXTREMISTS NOT RECOGNISED.
LORD R CECIL'S STATEMENT.

Reuter's representative last night had an interview with Lord Robert Cecil, who made the following statement on the Russian situation:

I do not believe that the action just taken by the Extremists in Petrograd really represents the views of the Russian people. It would, of course, be a direct breach of the agreement of September 5, 1914, and would mean not only that one ally had broken with the rest of its co-belligerents in the middle of the war, but had done so in the teeth of an express engagement to the contrary. Such action, if approved and adopted by the Russian nation, would put them practically outside the pale of the ordinary councils of Europe.

But I do not believe that the Russian people will confirm this action or approve a proclamation by those who profess to be the Government inciting soldiers to arrest their generals and to open all along the line peace negotiations with the enemy across the trenches. If this has for its object primarily the destruction of the Russian army as a fighting force it is difficult to see what other or more suitable steps could have been taken by those responsible in Petrograd.

As to recognition, while it is quite impossible to avoid a certain amount of business dealings, such, for instance, as questions arising out of the arrest of British subjects, there can be no question of diplomatic recognition or dealings with them. There is no intention of recognising such a Government.

2 The Secret Treaties

Of the various decrees passed either immediately by the Second Congress of Soviets on November 7 and 8, or by the newly elected Council of Peoples' Commissars, the most immediately menacing and calamitous to ruling circles in Britain was the *Decree on Peace*; and still more the steps taken to implement that decree. Day by day it was hoped that surely the Soviet Government would not carry out this outrageous flouting of the understanding between the Allies. But then there came the announcement that the Bolsheviks had found copies of the Secret Treaties between the Allies and that they would immediately destroy their secrecy and make them public to the whole world. This in particular seems to have filled the British and French foreign offices with the utmost degree of horror. When in one British morning newspaper, hitherto considered reputable, actual publication began of the text of the Secret Treaties, it was felt that the matter had gone so far that no further comment was possible except the comment of silence, the comment of refusal to mention the matter. When in the House of Commons it was asked was the Minister aware of publication in the *Manchester Guardian*, Foreign Secretary A J Balfour replied, with all the skill of one who had been Tory Prime Minister for many years, that he was aware of it, but that he did not propose to reveal those treaties himself and he would ignore the fact that they had in this manner been completely revealed.

What did these Secret Treaties (published in *Izvestia*, the organ of the Soviet, and *Pravda*, the organ of the Bolshevik Party, on November 23, 1917) contain? They were a first instalment of documents embodying agreements between the Allied or Entente Powers, made mainly in 1915 but confirmed as late as January 30 and

February 14 and 24, 1917. Foreign Minister Pokrovsky, the very last to hold that office, who had presided at the Allied conference from January 29 to February 21, recorded confidentially on February 12, 1917, for the benefit of the Tsar's ambassadors in Paris and London, that:

> "At an audience with the Most High, M Doumergue submitted to the Emperor the desire of France to secure for herself at the end of the present war the restoration of Alsace-Lorraine and a special position in the valley of the River Saar as well as to attain the political separation from Germany of her trans-Rhenish districts and their organisation on a separate basis in order that in future the River Rhine might form a permanent strategical frontier against a Germanic invasion …. His Imperial Majesty was pleased to agree with this in principle."

Pokrovsky added a reminder of the standpoint of the Tsar's Government (in the telegram of February 24, 1916) to the effect that "while allowing France and England complete liberty in delimiting the western frontier of Germany, we expect that the Allies on their part will give us equal liberty in delimiting our frontiers with Germany and Austro-Hungary". Two days later a Note of the Minister of Foreign Affairs, on February 14, 1917, to Maurice Paléologue, the French Ambassador in Petrograd, solemnised the matter thus:

> "By order of his Imperial Majesty, my most august master, I have the honour, in the name of the Russian Government, to inform your Excellency by the present Note that the Government of the Republic may rely upon the support of the Imperial Government for the carrying out of its plans as set out above." (*Manchester Guardian*, December 12, 1917)

At an earlier stage, towards the end of 1916, the British Foreign Office had privately elaborated proposals for "the creation of a Polish Kingdom" which would include much of the Polish population then within Germany as well as the Silesian coalfields and would be ruled by a member of the Russian Royal Family – "under a Russian Grand Duke". On this, however, the instruction from Petrograd to the ambassador in Paris on March 9 began as follows:

> "The political agreements concluded between the Allies during the war must remain intact, and are not subject to revision".

And then (as though the Tsar's ministers had an inkling of what was in the British Foreign Office's memorandum) it stated:

> "It is particularly necessary to insist on the exclusion of the Polish question from

the subjects of international discussion and on the elimination of all attempts to place the future of Poland under the guarantee and the control of the Powers."

The *Manchester Guardian* quoted the provisions for the division of the Ottoman Empire, of the Middle East, of Persia and of the Afghan frontiers.

Manchester Guardian, Wednesday, December 12, 1917:
"The Imperial Government completely shares the view of the British Government that the holy Moslem places must also in future remain under an independent Moslem rule. It is desirable to elucidate at once whether it is contemplated to leave those places under the rule of Turkey, the Sultan retaining the title of Caliph, or to create new independent States, since the Imperial Government would only be able to formulate its desires in accordance with one or other of these assumptions. On its part the Imperial Government would regard the separation of the Caliphate from Turkey as very desirable. Of course the freedom of pilgrimage must be completely secured.

"The Imperial Government confirms its assent to the inclusion of the neutral zone of Persia in the British sphere of influence. At the same time, however, it regards it as just to stipulate that the districts adjoining the cities of Ispahan and Yezd, forming with them one inseparable whole, should be secured for Russia in view of the Russian interests which have arisen there. The neutral zone now forms a wedge between the Russian and Afghan frontiers, and comes up to the very frontier line of Russia at Tulgager. Hence a portion of this wedge will have to be annexed to the Russian sphere of influence. Of essential importance is the question of railway construction in the neutral zone, which will require further amicable discussion."

Another secret document, dated March 7, 1915, was now given to the world. It was concerned with the claim of the Tsar to Constantinople, the Straits – the price of Russian support for British and French claims on the Ottoman Empire. Some small territories and towns near Lake Van and Mount Ararat, together with Erzeroum and Trebizond, were also to be carved out of the body of Turkey and given to the Tsar. But Britain was to have the lion's share, both in the valley of the Euphrates and Tigris, then called Mesopotamia and now Iraq, and also in Palestine. The Ottoman Empire was to be torn up. Britain, which was also to get as mandated territories the lion's share of colonies in Africa, in the meantime had, by the Sykes-Picot agreement, portioned out Syria and the Lebanon to be the French share of the booty, while British agents such as T E Lawrence had assured the Arabs that Syria would be theirs.

These revelations of what the Allies had secretly agreed upon showed that in every country blood was being shed for the sake of territorial aggression and expansion.

In Britain these disclosures had an immediate effect, which was driven home in the anti-war weekly press, both socialist and pacifist. They were talked about in the workshops and began to seep through everywhere. It put an edge on every agitation, local or national, economic or political. This in turn reacted on the government.

3   The blanket of the dark

Already in November 1917 it began to be realised that the stream of news flowing from Russia was not only meagre but tainted and unreliable.[3] It was tainted at the source. Diplomats and journalists, all anti-Bolshevik, sent telegrams conveying what they themselves believed – or what they thought should be believed in order to bolster war-time morale. Consequently what had been news in the sense of an endeavour to give a truthful account of the facts turned into the semblance of a war communiqué. The war communiqué was deservedly suspect, either because it lied or for its significant suppression of essential facts.

From the time the Soviets published their call for peace, and disclosed the Secret Treaties, despatches about Russia began to take on a quality of inventive falsification. No rumour was too absurd, no accusation too revolting but that it was alleged against the Bolsheviks. Lord Ponsonby, in his *Falsehood in War-Time*, exposed dozens of 'atrocities', purely imaginary, which had been fed to the eyes and ears of the British public in order to stimulate hatred of the German enemy in the 1914-18 war; had he attempted a similar exposure of lies circulated throughout the nations against the Bolsheviks, he would soon have completely lost count of them.

The process began with suppression of news. In the week that *Izvestia* and *Pravda* began publication of the Secret Treaties, one of the five members of the War Cabinet had put a stop to publication, or indeed transmission, of wireless messages from Russia. This was Sir Edward Carson, who then brought the matter up at the War Cabinet on Thursday November 29. He had a letter from Sir Frank Swettenham, Joint Director from 1915 to 1919 of the Official Press Bureau, about press messages on Russian affairs. This put the request,

> "pass, stop, or censor all such messages at our discretion, without regard to existing instructions that cablegrams dealing with foreign affairs are to be passed to the addressees uncensored".

The War Cabinet minute (*WC286*) records the discussion that followed:

> "Sir Edward Carson explained that some of the messages were appeals to the people as against their Governments, and were in many respects of a violent character. He had discussed the question with Mr Balfour and Lord Milner before their departure for Paris, and they were against publication."

Lord Robert Cecil, who was present as Minister of Blockade, demurred, saying:

> "it was better to throw the onus on to the Press and let them risk prosecution under the Defence of the Realm Act".

But the others were for direct suppression, and so

> "The War Cabinet decided that:
> "For the present the messages above referred to should not be published, and that the Press Bureau should be allowed to show the messages to the newspapers to which they were addressed, at their discretion."

This anti-enemy technique, but if anything intensified, was now applied against the country Russia which had been an ally in the war. Three years later Walter Lippman and Charles Merz wrote a supplement to *The New Republic* (August 4, 1920) entitled 'A Test of the News' in which they listed a series of invented atrocities and other falsehoods that had been printed in the *New York Times* from March 1917 to March 1920. Amongst other such cock-and-bull stories was the infamous invention in 1918 about 'Nationalisation of Women', which then became the horrifying headline, especially in Sunday papers.

The blanket of the dark came down on what was happening inside that nearly one-sixth of the world that had been Tsarist Russia. It did not fall immediately, because the Russian wireless news was printed for a fortnight or so. During the armistice and peace negotiations some publicity was allowed. But from the spring onwards of 1918 the sources of news that were not tainted were closed down one by one; there ceased to be any possibility of getting the same sort of information, however incomplete and biased, as had been available in the first stage from February 1917 inwards.

This 'poisoning of the wells' particularly affected the 'Left' weekly papers, organs of opinion, whose comment was dependent on what was available in the daily newspapers. Censorship plus this 'Blanket of the Dark' made it hard for them to get a clear notion of what was happening. The consequence was a considerable degree of confusion: they were often misled by seemingly genuine reports which turned out afterwards to have little or no foundation. In some cases the confusion was purely subjective and due to an unclear political understanding or outlook.

4 Specimen of a socialist paper

What were the main standpoints on the October Revolution of the Labour and socialist press? It will be remembered that this weekly press could be divided broadly into two sections. One section had joined in the *union sacré* of political parties for the waging of the war. This broadly covered: *Justice*, by then organ of the National Democratic Party; *The Clarion*, still edited by Robert Blatchford, who was now devoting himself to frenzied attacks on shop stewards such as William Gallacher; the *New Age*, once a Left-wing paper; and finally the *New Statesman*, initiated by Fabian leaders in 1913, and now under the editorship of Clifford Sharp. This last exhibited frequent leanings towards the Liberal Government so long as H H Asquith was Prime Minister. All of these papers were against the October Revolution, reheating opinion within the party with which they were connected. This was true, even if in the Fabian Society Bernard Shaw had expressed some solidarity in his remark about the Bolsheviks: "They are Socialists: we are Socialists. We must be on their side." Thus the pro-war section, all of them, were against the Proletarian Socialist Revolution. The others, as we shall see, were not all of a piece.

The Call, a fortnightly publication of the British Socialist Party, wrote on November 29 that "genuine and not make-believe Socialists have seized the reins of power", and praised the Bolsheviks for "courageous loyalty to the principles of International Socialism as laid down, for the time of war, by the Stuttgart and Basle Congresses". *The Socialist* wrote in December: "We of the SLP send our greetings to the Russian Maximalists and wish them success. Our Russian comrades have set about stopping the war in the right way." In an editorial on November 17, on 'the Lenin Revolution', *Workers' Dreadnought* wrote that "the Russian Revolution is a Socialist Revolution".

But probably the most influential at this time of the weekly socialist press that was critical of the coalition government was the *Herald*, edited by George Lansbury. Like most British weeklies of the Left, it often had a mixture of unreconciled standpoints; there was "something in it for everybody". In the cant phrase of a later day the paper was, like *Forward* in Glasgow, "an open forum". Its outstanding contributor especially on international affairs was H N Brailsford whose *War of Steel and Gold*, published early in 1914, had thrust him into the front rank of socialist writers and theoreticians.[4]

Brailsford, who had uttered warnings in advance about the war, was in favour of bringing the war to an end as soon as possible. How then, did Brailsford react to the Soviet standpoint on peace and *The Call* for a general armistice? In the *Herald* of December 1, 1917, his article headed 'A Separate Peace?' began by expressing his revulsion against the Bolsheviks:

> "They swore that they would make no peace with Emperor or Kaiser – the *Daily Mail* swore no harder – and even prayed of conducting a universal war against all capitalistic empires. All this, it seems, was demagogic froth. They are now trying to arrange a separate truce with the enemy, and, if it fails, the fault will not lie with Lenin and Trotsky."

The effort, repeated steadily from November until the end of the year 1917, and even thereafter, to bring a cessation of hostilities on all fronts as a preliminary to peace and to the release of mankind from the horrors of war, was brushed aside by Brailsford who went on to say:

> "The Bolsheviks ignore the Pact of London, which binds the Allies to make war and peace in common."

That was the Tsar's doing, but in Brailsford's view was nonetheless the kind of obligation which descended to his successors; for although the Russian people were assuredly not bound by the Secret Treaties, they had all the same "an overwhelming moral obligation, deeper and stronger than any treaty". The socialist Brailsford, oblivious at this point that he was copying the sentiments of Sir Edward Grey on August 4, 1914 as he launched the people of Britain into the World War without actually being bound by treaty, wrote that the Russian people was "bound in honour to the peoples who went to war at its side, to Belgium, to Serbia, to Roumania, to France".

Returning to the subject of the Bolsheviks, Brailsford wrote sternly:

> "They are putting themselves outside the pale of our International Socialist Society."

Here the Socialist opponent of the Government was simply parroting the remark made by the Tory Under-Secretary for Foreign Affairs, Lord Robert Cecil, a week before on November 23, 1917.

Not until a fortnight later could an answer to Brailsford appear. Then in the *Herald* of December 15, an article entitled 'Bolsheviks and Peace' argued that there was no warrant for the view that the Bolsheviks were placing themselves "outside the pale" but that:

> "On the contrary, it would seem that the Bolsheviks are more concerned to foster the growth of that International Socialist Society than anyone else in Europe."

The article, which had been conveyed out of prison, after a remark that "no paper in this country has so far endeavoured to have a sympathetic understanding of the position", referred to the full text of the Bolshevik appeal to belligerents (published the previous week in the *Labour Leader*) which made it clear that "the Bolsheviks are still endeavouring to attain general peace, and that the armistice has been initiated with this object". Remarks of a more excoriating nature such as that it was Brailsford who now was behaving like one of Northcliffe's *Daily Mail* scribes, were cut out by the editor.[5]

This specimen given in detail illustrates the peculiar collapse of a revered guru of socialist doctrines, when confronted by something that was real, namely, the Proletarian Socialist Revolution.[6]

5   Brest-Litovsk

To the call from the Soviet Government for a ceasefire on all fronts and then immediate peace talks, the Allies did not deign to reply. The German Chancellor Graf von Hertling in a speech to the Reichstag a week later (November 29) declared, however, that he accepted the peace formula. On this basis the Soviet Government negotiated first a truce then a formal armistice and finally to enter on peace negotiations with the representatives of the Central Empires. Each stage of the negotiations, it was insisted by the Russians, was to be public and transmitted to the world over the wireless. Between each stage they notified the Allies of the progress of these negotiations; the truce negotiations were interrupted for a week to enable the Allies to take part. And the Soviet Note of December 6 said "in case of a refusal they must declare clearly and definitely before all mankind the aims for which the people of Europe may have to lose their blood during a fourth year of the war". Again, on December 17, the Allied embassies in Petrograd were notified of the armistice to be followed soon by peace negotiations and were asked to participate. Even at the first day of peace negotiations, the Russians proposed a fortnight's adjournment to enable the new principles of peace to be communicated to all the belligerent powers in order that general peace negotiations might start on this basis. It was clear that negotiations for a separate peace would begin in January 1918 only if the Allies refused to participate.

The peace conference opened at Brest-Litovsk on December 22, 1917. It was attended by the Soviet delegation and those of the quadruple alliance, namely, Germany, Austria-Hungary, Bulgaria and Turkey. At this first sitting the Soviet delegation put forward six peace points, being an expansion of the formula "no annexations, no indemnities".

The impact as the peace negotiations began, and as the "beyond the pale" Soviet Government showed no sign whatever of being overthrown from within, shook the world of diplomacy to its foundations. The Soviet Six Peace Points, following upon the publication of the Secret Treaties, inevitably raised everywhere in the belligerent countries the question: what are the war aims? Only two weeks after the peace talks had begun, President Woodrow Wilson put forward his famous "Fourteen Points". On January 7, 1918 he addressed the United States Congress and referred to the parleys in progress at Brest-Litovsk and praised the Russians, saying:

"The Russian representatives have insisted very justly, very wisely, and in the true spirit of modern democracy, that the conferences they have been holding with the Teutonic and Turkish statesmen should be held with open, not closed doors. And all the world has been audience, as they desired."

President Woodrow Wilson then went on to say,

> "There is, moreover, a voice calling for the definitions of principle and of purpose …. It is the voice of the Russian people."

To this he proposed "to respond with utter sincerity and frankness".

Then came the famous Fourteen Points, beginning with "Open covenants of peace, openly arrived at", and amongst them the sixth point, the famous "Acid Test":

> "The evacuation of all Russian territory and such a settlement of all questions affecting Russia as will secure the best and freest cooperation of the other nations of the world in obtaining for her an unembarrassed and unhampered opportunity for the independent determination of her political development and national policy, and assure her of a sincere welcome into the society of free nations under institutions of her own choosing; and, more than a welcome, assistance also of every kind that she may need and may herself desire. The treatment accorded Russia by her sister nations in the months to come will be the acid test of their goodwill, of their appreciation of her needs as distinguished from their own interests, and of their intelligent and unselfish sympathy."

What was the precise value of this sixth point, the "Acid Test"? How did it square with the refusal of the American ambassador and the other ambassadors of the Entente powers to recognise or hold any communications with the Soviet Government? The 14 Points of President Woodrow Wilson undoubtedly had the effect of reassuring people in every country who had been seriously perturbed by the revelation of the Secret Treaties of the real aims for which they were being asked to make sacrifices and, if need be, give up their lives. The 14 Points had, as is known, considerable effect within Germany and Austria-Hungary. It did not however mean that any steps were taken by the United States to carry out the policy of the Acid Test.

Meantime at Brest-Litovsk the discussion continued of the Six Peace Points, "no annexations, no indemnities". At first the Central Powers' representatives appeared to agree with this declaration. Ten days after President Wilson's speech, however, on January 18, they made known their Governments' territorial claims. This included the seizure of Poland, Lithuania, some of Estonia and Latvia and other parts. There were discussions in Petrograd. Lenin instructed Trotsky, then People's Commissar for Foreign Affairs, to drag out the talks to the utmost, but to sign a peace treaty in the event of a German ultimatum. The talks were resumed on January 30. On February 9 the Austrian and German delegations concluded a secret treaty with the representatives of the Ukrainian Rada which actually gave Germany leave to plunder the Ukraine. Then the German delegation demanded that the talks be speeded up. On February 10 the Soviet delegation asked for instructions and Lenin reaffirmed his earlier instruction. Trotsky however issued a statement that Russia would not sign such a peace treaty, but would discontinue the war and demobilise the army; there would be "neither war nor peace". The talks broke down.

On February 18 the Germans started an offensive along the whole front. On the morning of February 19 a wireless message was sent to the German Government stating the Soviet Government's willingness to sign peace on the German terms set forth at Brest-Litovsk. The German Command's reply, received on February 23, contained terms which were far more onerous. They had to be accepted. The treaty was signed on March 3. These negotiations at Brest-Litovsk were conducted publicly and were reported over the wireless. Consequently they were heard in every country and, except to the extent that a censorship prevented or mangled the reports, they became available to the peoples.

The United States was not an Allied but an associated power. Though the United States' ambassador in Russia gave no recognition, nevertheless President Woodrow Wilson sent the following message to the meeting of the Third Congress of Soviets on March 11, 1918:

"May I not take advantage of the Congress of the Soviets to express the sincere sympathy which the people of the United States feel for the Russian people at this moment when the German power had been thrust in to interrupt and turn back the whole struggle for freedom and substitute the wishes of Germany for the purposes of the people of Russia? Although the Government of the United States is, unhappily, not now in a position to render the direct and effective aid it would wish to render, I beg to assure the people of Russia through the Congress that it will avail itself of every opportunity to secure for Russia once more complete sovereignty and independence in her own affairs, and full restoration to her great role in the life of Europe and the modern world. The whole heart of the people of the United States is with the people of Russia in the attempt to free themselves forever from autocratic Government and become master of their own lives."

To this the Congress of Soviets sent the following reply:

"The Congress expresses its gratitude to the American people, above all to the labouring and exploited masses of the United States, for the sympathy expressed to the Russian people by President Wilson through the Congress of Soviets in the days of severe trials.

"The Russian Socialist Federative Republic of Soviets takes advantage of President Wilson's communication to express to all peoples perishing and suffering from the horrors of imperialistic war its warm sympathy and firm belief that the happy time is not far distant when the labouring masses of all countries will throw off the yoke of capitalism and will establish a Socialist state of society, which alone is capable of securing a just and lasting peace as well as the culture and well-being of all labouring people."

6 Attitude of the United Kingdom Government

Meanwhile the attitude of the British Government presented, in the mouths of its spokesmen, no such apparent ambiguity as in the words uttered by the President of the USA from mid-December to mid-March 1918. But this does not mean that its attitude was fully stated. Its extreme hostility to the Proletarian Socialist Revolution was made clear from the very beginning, directly and through its agents; but how that hostility was to be manifested and into what policy it would issue was not immediately clear. Nor was it known that the Foreign Office had taken a standpoint which was the prelude to the armed intervention to be carried out in the spring and summer of 1918. Lord Balfour, formerly Conservative Prime Minister from 1902 to 1905, had been responsible for a memorandum adopted by the Cabinet on December 21, 1917, the day before the Brest-Litovsk talks began. It contained the following statements:

> "We should represent to the Bolsheviks that we have no desire to take part in any way in the internal politics of Russia, and that any idea that we favour a counter-revolution is a profound mistake. Such a policy might be attractive to the autocratic Governments of Germany and Austria, but not to the Western democracies or America. ...
>
> "The first thing is money to reorganise the Ukraine, to pay the Cossacks and Caucasian forces and to subsidise the Persians. ...
>
> "If the French could undertake the finance of the Ukraine, we might find the money for the others. It is understood that the United States will assist. Besides finance, it is important to have agents and officers to advise and support the provincial Governments and their armies. It is essential that this should be done as quietly as possible, so as to avoid the imputation – as far as we can – that we are preparing to make war on the Bolsheviks."

If from a country's reams of state papers there were to be picked out examples that would justify the continental description of British foreign policy as that of 'perfide Albion' then this one should surely stand high on the list. It was of course a clear intimation to those who read it in the Cabinet and were accustomed to this 'Aesopean' language that they were preparing and, had in hand, full preparations for making war on the Bolsheviks. For this is what they did, in 1918, in 1919 and in 1920.

Meantime, however, the refusal to have any contact with the Bolsheviks, the treatment of the Soviet Government as a leper, an untouchable, had some minor awkward consequences. There was the question of visas, and the position of British people inside the Soviet borders. Consequently it was thought convenient to arrange to have a British Diplomatic Agent to go to Moscow – which implied in turn the recognition of a Soviet representative in Britain. However unwillingly, the latter had to be agreed to. At first it had appeared that this might be no other than Georgy Chicherin, then held in prison. On the insistence of the Soviet Government he, together with another Russian, was released and taken over to Russia, where in the spring of 1918 he became People's Commissar of Foreign Affairs. Bruce Lockhart, previously British Consul General in Moscow, was to be the British Agent. The Soviet choice was Maxim Litvinov, who had for a considerable time represented the Bolshevik Party in Britain and, for example, had been their representative at the attempt (which he denounced) to hold an "Allied Socialist" conference in London early in 1915. Litvonov, already fairly well-known in England, being married to an Englishwoman, the daughter of a well-known professor, became the representative of the Bolsheviks, while a Tsarist chargé d'affaires still was recognised and inhabited the Russian Embassy. Similarly the opportunity was taken to nominate as Soviet Consul in Glasgow no other than John Maclean, who earlier that year had been released from prison where he was serving a long sentence. He had been rescued, like the framed-up Tom Mooney in the United States, by the agitation.

The growing agitation in the workshops had centred round economic demands. There were threats of strikes because of the rising cost of living, food shortages, tighter restrictions in the Military Services Acts and in the stiffened Defence of the Realm Act. Winston Churchill as Minister of Munitions raised the question in the Government that some statements of policy must be made to counteract the effect of the Russian Revolution in the workshops of the vast munitions industry.

Prime Minister Lloyd George relates how in the winter of 1917,

> "the determination of the Russian workers and peasants to make peace on the basis of 'no annexation and no indemnities' was also having its effect on public opinion amongst a considerable section of the industrial population in Britain and France"

and, he added,

> "the attitude of the Workers' Government in Russia was having a very disturbing effect on the artisans in our workshops".[7]

7   Litvinov at Nottingham

When the Labour Party Conference was held on January 23-25, 1918, to consider the reorganisation of the Labour Party together with a new programme, Litvinov was invited to Nottingham as representative of the Bolshevik section of the Russian Social Democratic Labour Party. On December 28 the British "Memorandum on War Aims" had been approved at a special joint conference of the Labour Party and the British Trades Union Congress. These then called together a conference of Allied Labour and Socialist parties to see whether agreement could be reached on the memorandum. This was termed the Third Inter-Allied Conference and was to be held on February 20, 1918. They invited the Labour and Socialist organisations of all the countries allied to the British Government. They invited the Russian parties affiliated to the Socialist International, namely, the Socialist Revolutionary Party and the Russian Social Democratic Labour Party (both Bolshevik and Menshevik sections). The American Federation of Labor refused to come on the ground that the conference was linked up with the Stockholm Project to which they were opposed. The Bolsheviks also refused to come because they could not accept an invitation to a conference of so sectional a nature which was opposed to the principles of international socialism.

On the evening before the conference, on January 22, Litvinov addressed a special meeting of delegates who were ready to hear fraternal delegates. It is recorded that Litvinov as the diplomatic representative of the first Workers' Republic was given an extremely warm and friendly reception, at any rate from the gallery. Litvinov, speaking in English, said:

> "I am the representative of no ordinary Government. For the first time the working classes have attained supreme power in one of the largest states in the world. The significance of events in Russia has been beclouded by the war and by misrepresentations. I appeal to the British workers to disabuse their minds of the notion that the Bolsheviks have usurped power like a band of conspirators."

The Russian toilers, he said, wanted peace as well as freedom and social reforms. They revolted, not against the unsuccessful conduct of the war, but against the war itself. He went on to explain and to ask a question: Had the experience of the Revolution justified itself? The answer was, in one word – Brest-Litovsk. Even if peace did not result from the negotiations, a revolution in Germany and perhaps somewhere else might come within the range of immediate possibilities. He then alluded to trouble inside Germany:

> "Will the German people continue to shed their blood to encourage their

Junkers and capitalists? I think there can be only one answer. Already we hear the rumblings of the storm coming from Austria and Hungary. It will, no doubt, also spread over Germany."

It was true enough. The effect of conditions inside Germany together with the wireless propaganda of the Bolsheviks at Brest-Litovsk resulted in a series of strikes in the capitals of Germany, Hungary and Austria, culminating in very serious stoppages on the last day of January 1918.

It was perhaps as an offset to this speech that 5 months later, at the Conference of the Labour Party on June 26-28, Arthur Henderson, leader of the Labour Party, and still strongly in favour of the war policy, invited Alexander Kerensky to attend the conference as a fraternal delegate. Kerensky was given the most flattering reception in the bourgeois Press for his speech; but he did not please the Labour delegates to anything like the extent that he pleased the bourgeoisie. Throughout Britain anti-war feeling was beginning to mount. The demand for peace was growing. It might take the form only of a demand in the first place for a negotiated peace as against the Lloyd George policy of a "knock-out blow"; but amongst the mass of the people the demand was growing. There was the evidence also that in the weekly socialist papers there was now a growing support for the Proletarian Socialist Revolution in Russia.

Lenin, speaking at the Congress of Soviets in March was able then (and still more in his letter to American workers) to claim with justification that the first 5 months since November 7 had shown the triumphal progress of the Revolution and its complete acceptance throughout all of Russia.

Notes and References

1 In the jungle of thick-coming fancies that invaded the minds of the British bourgeoisie there inevitably sprouted mythologies. Much as medieval Englishmen feared the fabled deities of the Saracens, Mahound and Termagant, so their descendants believed in a two-headed demon, called Lenin-and-Trotsky, who with its 'squads of Chinese executioners' (collectively known as 'The Bolshies') was responsible for all the ills that were to affect mankind. For writers and orators in the capitalist countries, for politicians and parsons alike, the Russian Revolution was thus personalised as Evil incarnate in an unholy Duality. The origin of this particular myth may have lain partly in the fact that Trotsky, as first to be in charge of foreign affairs, was brought into closer contact with diplomats and journalists from outside Russia and partly in his highly photogenic features and seductive style of phrasemaking.

2 "Commissaries" was the first, and perfectly correct, use in the English language of the Russian word Komissar, itself borrowed from the *Commissaires* 125 years earlier in the French Revolution, which in turn may well have been taken from the English Revolution where in the New Model Army regiments elected "agitators" in whose debates at Putney in 1649 General Henry Ireton is addressed as "Commissary" while Oliver Cromwell is "Commissary General".

3 "The news from Russia is scanty and is evidently biased and unreliable." (*Labour Leader*, November 15, 1917)

4 The eclecticism of the paper was not much diminished by caveats appended to anti-Bolshevik articles in such terms as "Our readers will understand that Mr Brailsford is expressing his own views, which are not

necessarily ours. *–Ed.* Herald."

5   This article appeared under the nom de plume of ABH; it was written by the author, who was in jail as a war resister.

6   Exactly 6 years later Brailsford made noble amends by his preface to *Nailed to the Counter: a Record of Misrepresentation concerning Soviet Russia* (the Labour Publishing Company, London 1923).

7   D Lloyd George, *The Truth about the Peace Treaties*, Vol 1, Gollancz, London, pp 66-7 *–Ed.*

Appendix I

Wireless and *Reuter* messages in fourth week of November 1917

Manchester Guardian, Thursday, November 22, 1917
RUSSIAN ARMISTICE OFFERED.
INSTRUCTIONS ISSUED.

The following, transmitted through the wireless stations of the Russian Government, would appear to be a message sent to the Commander-in-Chief of the Russian armies:

By the order of the All Russian Congress of Workmen's and Soldiers' Delegates, the Council of the People's Commissaries has taken power into its hands, together with the obligation to offer to all the peoples and their respective Governments an immediate armistice on all fronts, with the purpose of immediately opening pourparlers for the conclusion of a democratic peace.

When the power of the Council is firmly established in all the most important places of the country the Council of the People's Commissaries will make without delay a formal offer of armistice to all the nations involved in the war, to the Allies and also to the nations at war with us.

A draft of this message to this effect has been sent to all the People's Commissaries for Foreign Affairs and to all the plenipotentiary representatives of the Allied nations in Petrograd.

To you, Citizen Commander-in-Chief, the Council of the People's Commissaries, in fulfilling the resolution of the Congress of the Workmen's and Soldiers' Delegates, orders that after receiving the present message you shall approach the commanding authorities of the enemy armies with an offer of a cessation of all hostile activities for the purpose of opening peace pourparlers.

In charging you with the conduct of these preliminary pourparlers the Council of the People's Commissaries orders you: (1) to keep the Council constantly informed by direct wire of all your pourparlers with the enemy armies; (2) to sign the preliminary act only after the approval by the Council of the People's Commissaries.

(Signed)
VLADIMIR OULIANOFF LENIN, President of the Council of the People's Commissaries.
L TROTSKY, Commissary for Foreign Affairs
N KRYLENKO, Commissary for the War
VLADIMIR BONTCH BRUEVITCH, Chairman of the Council
N GORBOUNOV, Secretary

Manchester Guardian, Saturday, November 24, 1917
THE PEACE PROPOSALS.
ARMY FORMING A NEW GOVERNMENT.
Petrograd, Wednesday.

M Trotsky, the Bolshevik Foreign Minister, has written to the Allies' representatives informing them of the organisation of the new Government of the Russian Republic, and requesting the Ambassadors and Ministers to regard the proposals for a truce and a democratic peace approved by the all-Russia Congress as a formal proposal for an immediate truce on all fronts, and for the immediate opening of peace negotiations.

M Trotsky states that this proposal has been addressed simultaneously to all the peoples and Governments at war. M Trotsky announces that it will be published immediately.

The "Dyelo Naroda" learns that the army committees at the front are taking the initiative in the formation of a new Government in which all Socialist parties will be represented, with the following "platform":

1. The immediate handing over of the land to Land Committees.
2. The meeting of the Constituent Assembly at a date to be fixed.
3. Abolition of the political "Terror" and restoration of civic liberties.

The Revolutionary Committee in Moscow is reported to have seized a branch of the State Bank, whither, it is added, one hundred roubles were recently transferred from Petrograd. Commissioner Lunacharsky admits that two million roubles worth of valuables were stolen from the Winter Palace after its capture by the Maximalists.

Admiral Verderevsky, Minister of Marine in the Kerensky Cabinet, is relinquishing his Ministry.

The Congress of Peasants' Delegates is transferring its seat to Mohileff from Petrograd owing to the apprehension of Maximalist intervention and for the purpose of enabling the soldiers at the front to participate in its meetings. –*Reuter*.

Appendix II

War Cabinet on General Policies towards Russia

Russia

6. With reference to War Cabinet 279, Minute 16, the War Cabinet discussed how far it was possible for the Allies to take any effective action in Russia against the Bolsheviks, who had now issued a wireless to the world announcing that they were determined on an armistice. It was pointed out that the Allied Governments had not so far recognised Lenin and his associates as a Russian Government, and could not recognise as an Allied Government in Russia any Government which officially put forward to the enemy proposals for peace. The difficulty was that any overt official step taken against the Bolsheviks might only strengthen their determination to make peace, and might be used to inflame anti-Allied feeling in Russia, and so defeat the very object we were aiming at. Nor was anything known of the actual position which would justify us, at this juncture, in backing either Kaledin or any other leader of the party of law and order. It was suggested that steps should be taken to build up in Russia some sort of unofficial organisation which could counter the work of the German organisation. Meanwhile, the best immediate step might be to let the Roumanians get into touch with General Kaledin, on purely military grounds, assuming, of course, that he was in a sufficiently strong position to help them. *(Thursday November 22, 1917, at 11.30 am)*

Russia: General Policy

15. The War Cabinet considered their general policy in regard to Russia and in this connection had before them a Memorandum by the Secretary of State for Foreign Affairs (Paper GT-2932), dated December 9, 1917 (Appendix).

It was suggested that His Majesty's Government was not primarily or specially concerned with the composition of the Russian Government, or with the local aspirations of the Bolsheviks or other political parties, except in so far as they bore in their attitude to our conflict with the Central Powers. This was the line we had taken during the Tsar's reign, and there was no reason to depart from it. Our dominant purpose throughout the revolution should be:

(a) If possible, to keep Russia in the war until our joint war aims were realised; or

(b) If this could not be secured, then to ensure that Russia was as helpful to us and as harmful to the enemy as possible. For this purpose we should seek to influence Russia to give to any terms of peace that might be concluded with the enemy a bias in our favour.

It was difficult to foretell how strong the Bolsheviks might become, or how long their power might endure; but if, as seemed likely, they maintained an ascendancy for the next few months only, these months were critical, and to antagonise them needlessly would be to throw them into the arms of Germany. There were at the moment signs that within a few days, when the elections for the Constituent Assembly had been completed, the Bolsheviks would be installed in power not only in a *de facto*, but also in a constitutional sense.

In this connection reference was made to a recent message which had been received from the British Embassy at Petrograd. In a telegram dated December 8, 1917 (Foreign Office No 1984), the terms were given of a six months' armistice proposed by the Bolsheviks, and it was stated that there was a remarkable change in the official Press, the Allies not being attacked, for the first time for several weeks.

In *The Times* of that day there appeared a report that the Germans were making the following conditions:

(a) Germany to obtain, for fifteen years, a control of the Russian wheat market.

(b) Importation into Russia of all German goods duty free.

(c) No territory now occupied by German troops to be surrendered.

Attention was also drawn to a telegram to the Chief of the Imperial General Staff, dated December 5, 1917 (No 1404), recounting a private and unofficial interview with Krylenko, the Bolshevik Commander-in-Chief of the Russian Army, during which he said that he had issued an order that all armistice agreements should contain a clause forbidding transfer of .troops from one front to another. He appeared most anxious to make a favourable impression on Allied officers, and had carried out all suggestions made to him for safeguarding the lives of officers and their families.

In a telegram dated December 6, 1917 (Foreign Office No 1971), Sir George Buchanan reported an interview between Captain Smith and Trotzki, at which the prohibition of British subjects leaving Russia was discussed in connection with the detention in this country of Messrs Chicherine and Petroff. Trotzki denied that the prohibition was intended as a threat. His object had been to emphasise the difference between the treatment accorded to Russian subjects in the United Kingdom and British subjects in Russia. On publication in the local press of a communiqué to the effect that the British Government would reconsider the cases of all Russian subjects interned in Great Britain and would give facilities for return to their country of all Russians innocent of any offences punishable by the laws of Great Britain, he (Trotzki) would the same day restore full liberty of movement to all British subjects in Russia. Sir George Buchanan urged His Majesty's Government to agree to accept the compromise proposed by Trotzki, otherwise he feared that British subjects would be held up indefinitely.

The War Cabinet were impressed with the fact that, by continuing to intern Chicherine and Petroff the lives of thousands of British subjects were being endangered, and that the case for their internment was not a very strong one. On the other hand, the dangers of any traffic with the Bolsheviks were very real. The strength of the Bolshevik Government lay in the fact that it supported peace, and that if it abandoned its efforts for peace it would probably be overthrown. Further, to take any action on the lines suggested above – action for which the Bolshevik Government had pressed – could hardly be regarded as consistent with the support which was being proffered to General Kaledin in the South. Was it desirable to treat with both Trotzki and Kaledin at one and the same time? Our policy towards Kaledin had been decided upon. Would it not be wise to wait and see whether the Bolshevik Government was going to last?

To this it was replied that our assistance to Kaledin was directed against the Bolsheviks, and was specially intended to help the Roumanians.

The War Cabinet, without making any change in their recent policy towards Russia, authorised –

The Secretary of Sate for Foreign Affairs to inform Sir George Buchanan that the policy proposed in his telegram No 1971 was accepted.

The Secretary of State for Foreign Affairs also undertook to deal with Chicherine and Petroff in the best way he could, in consultation with Sir George Buchanan and the Home Secretary, and to deal with three other Russians who were reported as having been interned here.

Appendix to December 10 War Cabinet
by AJ Balfour

Notes on the present Russian situation

As I may not be able to be present at Cabinet tomorrow, I desire to make these notes.

The following points have to be specially kept in view:

1. The safety of our Embassy in Petrograd and of British subjects in Russia.
2. The interests of Roumania and her army.
3. The best course to adopt in order to diminish as much as possible the advantage which Germany will be able to extract from the dissolution of the Russian army as a fighting force.

These subjects are all interconnected, though so far as possible I will deal with them separately.

1. The greatest danger to Sir George Buchanan and the British colony arises

probably out of the possibility of mob-violence, excited by the anti-British propaganda fomented by German money in Petrograd and elsewhere. The only real security against this is to be found either by the establishment of a strong and order-loving Government in Russia, or by the removal of the British, official and unofficial, to some safer country.

The first we can do nothing to secure. The second cannot be obtained unless we are able (a) to provide the necessary transport either through Sweden or through some northern port of Russia, and (b) to win the goodwill (in however qualified a form) of the present rulers of Petrograd.

The question of transport is hardly a Foreign Office matter, but the policy of avoiding the active malevolence of the Bolshevik party raises most important diplomatic issues.

It was suggested at Cabinet on Friday that, after their recent proclamation, the Bolsheviks could only be regarded as avowed enemies, and to treat them as anything else showed a lamentable incapacity to see facts as they are, and to handle them with decision.

I entirely dissent from this view and believe it to be founded on a misconception. If for the moment, the Bolsheviks show peculiar virulence in dealing with the British Empire, it is probably because they think that the British Empire is the great obstacle to immediate peace; but they are fanatics to whom the constitution of every Sate, whether monarchical or republican, is equally odious. Their appeal is to every revolutionary force, economic, social, racial, or religious, which can be used to upset the existing political organisations of mankind. If they summon the Mohammedans of India to revolt, they are still more desirous of engineering a revolution in Germany. They are dangerous dreamers, whose power, be it great or small, transitory or permanent, depends partly on German gold, partly on the determination of the Russian army to fight no more; but who would genuinely like to put into practice the wild theories which have so long been germinating in the shadow of the Russian autocracy.

Now, contrary to the opinion of some of my colleagues, I am clearly of opinion that it is to our advantage to avoid, as long as possible, an open breach with this crazy system. If this be drifting, then I am a drifter by deliberate policy. On the broader reasons for my view, I will say a word directly, but its bearing on the narrower issue of the safety of Sir George Buchanan and the British colony is evident. I am personally of opinion that the Cabinet should reverse the decision it came to some little time ago, and should deport to Russia the two interned Russian subjects in whose fate the Russian rulers appear to be so greatly interested. I was not in England when the decision to retain them was come to, and I am imperfectly acquainted with the reasons for it. Doubtless they were sufficient. But I certainly think that we may now with advantage send these two Russians back to their own country, where, judged by local standards, their opinions will probably appear sane and moderate.

I have already instructed Sir George Buchanan to abstain completely from any action which can be interpreted as an undue interference with the internal affairs of the country to which he is accredited, and I am unable to think of any other step which would help to secure his safety.

2. As regards the Roumanian army, events have marched rapidly. Everything that could be done, even as a forlorn hope, has been done to enable the army to join with other forces in Russia prepared to continue the struggle, but for the moment no such forces appear to exist, and the Roumanian army is under the strictest military necessity of acquiescing in the armistice, or rather the cessation of hostilities, on its part of the line. Very difficult and important questions, such as those raised by General Berthelot in a memorandum I have ordered to be circulated, still remain to be decided, but these call for no immediate action. I hope that General Berthelot's memorandum will be carefully considered by the Headquarters Staff.

3. I have already indicated my view that we ought if possible not to come to an open breach with the Bolsheviks or drive them into the enemy's camp. But there are wider reasons for this policy than the safety of the British colony in Russia. These wider reasons are as follows:

It is certain, I take it, that, for the remainder of this war, the Bolsheviks are going to fight neither Germany nor anyone else. But, if we can prevent their aiding Germany we do a great deal, and to this we should devote our efforts.

There are two possible advantages which Germany may extract from Russia's going out of the war: (i) She may increase her man-power in other theatres of operation by moving troops from the Russian front, or by getting back German prisoners. There is little hope of stopping this, and I say no more about it. (ii) She may obtain the power of using the large potential resources of Russia to break the Allied Blockade. I am not sure that this is not the more important of the two advantages, and it has so far been very imperfectly examined. As regards oil, we want to know what means of transport there is in the Black Sea available to the Germans, and how far the anti-Bolshevik elements in the Caucasian regions can be utilised to interfere with the supply on land. As regards cereals, the difficulties the Germans are likely to have arise mainly, I suppose, from the chaotic condition of the country, the disorganisation of all means of transport, and the determination of the Russians to use their own produce for their own purposes.

If we drive Russia into the hands of Germany, we shall hasten the organisation of the country by German officials on German lines. Nothing could be more fatal, it seems to me, both to the immediate conduct of the war and to our post-war relations.

Russia, however incapable of fighting, is not easily overrun. Except with the active goodwill of the Russians themselves, German troops (even if there were German troops to spare) are not going to penetrate many hundreds of miles into that vast country. A mere armistice between Russia and Germany may not for very many months promote in any important fashion the supply of German needs from Russian sources. It must be our business to make that period as long as possible by every means in our power, and no policy would be more fatal than to give the Russians a motive for welcoming into their midst German officials and German soldiers as friends and deliverers.

A J BALFOUR

Foreign Office, December 9, 1917

5 Intervention – 1918

1 Fourteen capitalist armies

With the acceptance in mid-March 1918 of the punitive peace of Brest-Litovsk by the Congress of Soviets, there came a certain change within Britain in the outlook both of the mass of the people and of the ruling circles. The hope that had been entertained by so many workers that the Brest-Litovsk negotiations would bring in their train universal peace was dashed to the ground. On the other hand it had become clear that within the borders of the territory the Revolution continued to be victorious. It had swept through all of old Russia from the Baltic to the Pacific Ocean. On the other hand the conclusion of the Brest-Litovsk peace, with its revelation of the extreme military weakness of the young revolutionary forces, was seized upon both by the Germans and their allies and by the British and their allies as giving the opportunity for intervention in the internal affairs of Russia in order to crush the Revolution.

There was nothing new in this in history. Revolutionary governments have more than once been assailed by the armed forces of existing states. The French Revolution had to face the armies simultaneously of 7 European powers. The Russian Revolution had to face simultaneously the armed forces of no less than 14 capitalist powers.

From the spring of 1918 hostilities and fighting continued right to the end of the year. For the first 6 months the Entente Powers and the Central Empires, though locked in deadly combat, seemed to have been actually cooperating objectively, at any rate, in their endeavour to weaken or crush the Bolsheviks. As to the German imperialists and their associates, they suppressed all socialist activities in the Baltic provinces. German support in Estonia and Latvia enabled counter-revolution to triumph. In Finland, German soldiers arrived to install a German princeling as monarch of Finland, leaving General Mannerheim as Regent, supported by German bayonets. The Ukraine was regarded by the Germans as a protectorate. They abolished the Ukrainian Rada, that evanescent government that had been recognised by them, and then by the Entente Powers, and put the Ukraine in the hands of the Hetman Skoropadsky under the surveillance of Field Marshall von Eichhorn. Then they pushed on beyond the Dnieper and the Don to the shores of the Black Sea, where the Soviet Government was compelled to sink the Black Sea Fleet to prevent it falling into the hands of the Germans. The Sultan of Turkey also intervened, pushing up into the Caucasus.

Without any detailed knowledge other than the usual rumours of what was happening within the borders of Russia, the Allies decided to request the Japanese to command forces in the far east of Siberia on the ground that the Japanese, according to Lord Balfour, "would be the friends and not the enemies of Russia". This was followed by British marines also landing at Vladivostok. In May 1918 a large force of Czechoslovak prisoners in Siberia were induced to revolt and seize the Trans-Siberian Railway, which they occupied eastwards, reaching Irkutsk on Lake Baikal by July 13. In June 1918 the British landed a force at Murmansk, ostensibly to prevent that coast from being used by the Germans as a base for submarines; but it was soon clear that the British authorities were hostile to the local Soviets. On August 2 they occupied Archangelsk and the mouth of the northern Dvina on the White Sea. They expelled the Bolsheviks and an anti-Bolshevik Government was set up and maintained by British bayonets. Presently the British force was reinforced by American soldiers at Archangelsk.

In the south the British force arrived at Baku on the Caspian Sea. Meantime the Japanese force which had occupied Vladivostok had advanced through the Far East and Siberia; while by the autumn an American contingent had also landed at Vladivostok and the British force accompanying the Japanese had reached beyond Irkutsk in Siberia.

By the middle of October 1918, supported and sustained by these troops of intervention, and heavily reinforced from all directions, local White Monarchist armies were set in motion; they were supplied, provisioned and munitioned by Britain and her allies against the Russian Revolution.

During all this late spring, summer and early autumn of 1918, right up to the Armistice which ended the First World War in November 1918, the survival of the Russian Revolution was in the balance.

What was the impact upon the working class in other countries, whose influence could have such a profound effect in staying the hands of the invaders of Russia? Those in the working class who had a mind to understand what was at stake and were ready to respond in the spirit of international socialism, understood that the utmost aid in action and patient explanation was called for.

Foremost amongst them were those in the socialist parties who fully accepted and understood the Revolution. Their influence was steadily exercised inside the workshops against the war and in favour of the Revolution.

Secondly, however, there was the wider circle they influenced and which was to be found in various parts throughout the British Labour movement, and which reached into the left wing of the Liberals who, though they were not in agreement or indeed wishing for any agreement with the Bolsheviks, were determinedly against intervention and rallied under the slogan, "Hands off Russia".

Lastly, there was the vast majority of the trade unions, the official organisations of the Labour movement. These, while utterly opposed to the Bolsheviks, were also opposed to the return of Tsardom, and feared that their own development to greater strength and weight within Britain would receive a fatal setback if the armies of intervention were successful in restoring autocratic rule.

With all these things operating, the tension between the pro-war and anti-war forces, between the socialists who accepted the standpoint of international socialism and those who were supporting the war aims of the coalition government, grew sharper and sharper.

There was more than one parallel to the events of the French Revolution in the attempt to crush the workers' republic by troops of intervention. As the forces of intervention began to cross Siberia and to approach the Urals the town council of Ekaterinburg (now Sverdlovsk) decided that it was necessary to deal with the Tsar Nicholas and his family who were imprisoned there, and in consequence executed them summarily in mid-July. Two months later in mid-September, a British force called the Dunster Force, pushing up from Persia and occupying the south of the Caspian Sea, brought Sepoy troops into the Trans-Caspian deserts and there in Turkmenistan were responsible for the execution or murder of 26 Bolshevik commissars in September.

The collapse of the German military and civil regime with the application on November 11, 1918 for an armistice and its conclusion, was followed nearly a month later by the abdication of the Kaiser in Berlin and the appointment of a new Chancellor. This had the following results. On the one hand it brought hostilities to an end. On the other the abdication of Wilhelm II, Kaiser of Germany, enabled the Soviet Union to annul the Treaty of Brest-Litovsk, and to begin taking back the territory of which they had been robbed in their western provinces. This, however, did not suit the book of the Allied interventionists who instructed the German generals (and repeated this instruction in the Armistice terms) that they were not to retire from Russian territory until they had made sure that the Red Army did not take over, but that some other force should do so, either local anti-Bolshevik capitalists or the British sailors or marines who were in charge of the Baltic provinces. Otherwise it seemed as though there would surely be an end to the intervention. Georgy Chicherin, Commissar for Foreign Affairs, on October 24 sent a message to the President of the United States saying:

> "The acid test of the relations between the United States and Russia has not given exactly the kind of results that one would have expected after your message to the Congress, Mr President. But we have cause to be not entirely dissatisfied even with these results, for the outrages of the counter-revolutionaries in the east and in the north have shown to the Russian working men and peasants what the Russian counter-revolution and its foreign supporters are aiming at, and as a result of this there have been created among the Russian masses an iron will to defend their freedom, to defend the conquests of the Revolution – the land which has now been given to the peasants, the factories which have now been given to the workers."

Meantime there was a short apparent pause. But it was a pause only before the renewal of the storm.

For the relaxation of German pressure was the signal for intensified attack by the Allied capitalist powers. No sooner was the armistice signed on November 11, 1918, than the French Fleet entered the Black Sea, transports were sent to Novorossiysk with military supplies for Denikin's army and several divisions of French troops were landed in the Crimea and at Odessa. The armistice had enabled the Allies to tackle still more seriously the military problem of conquering the Bolsheviks. The result was that by the end of the winter the situation of the Workers' Republic was hazardous. Not only were there these generals in the south, but in the north British forces and White troops with their puppet Government had moved south from Archangelsk. But as the spring approached the most formidable enemy of the republic appeared to be the forces under the command of Admiral Kolchak operating from Siberia.

2 The Armistice and after

Within days after the armistice had been signed on November 11, 1918, the decision was taken by the British government to hold the General Election as soon as possible. No time was lost and the election date was fixed for some three weeks ahead, in mid-December. The election was to be fought on a wide franchise. An extension of the franchise had been mooted and a committee had been appointed to work out proposals in 1916 well before the events of 1917. Therefore, contrary to what has sometimes been stated, the Representation of the People Act 1918, which doubled the number of voters in Britain and gave the vote to women over 30 years of age, was not itself the product of the impact of the Russian Revolution. Nevertheless there is no question that it received an impetus.

A hint of this was given when on March 19, 1917, Prime Minister Lloyd George was making his statement about the Russian Revolution and a Radical MP, Pringle, interjected the remark, "What about the reform of the franchise?" Further references were made in the House of Commons which make it unmistakably clear that the democratic upheaval that took place in 1917 had the constant effect of a reminder on the legislature which had been last elected in December 1910.

Amongst other proposals of a democratisation of the British franchise was the adoption of proportional representation. This was carried in the House of Commons and mangled and destroyed in the House of Lords. The Representation of the People Act 1918 reduced the residence qualification and enfranchised some categories of men who previously did not have the vote and, as said above, it enfranchised women over the age of 30.

The overwhelming victory of the coalition resulted, as Baldwin himself stated, in the return of a very large number of "hard-faced men who looked as if they had done well out of the war"; or, in other words, a pack of capitalist thieves and robbers. At the same time it made a clean sweep of the Left-wing. The leaders of the Labour Party who had been opposed to the war, or were even mildly critical of it and of the war effort led by Lloyd George, were swept out of Parliament. Ramsay MacDonald lost his seat, so did Philip Snowden, so did F W Jowett, and the only seat retained of that lot was W C Anderson. Besides these leaders of the Independent Labour Party there were a number of candidates of the British Socialist Party. and these too were defeated. Lastly, 3 candidates were put up by the Socialist Labour Party, who suffered defeat but received quite respectable votes. On the morrow of the election the candidates of what their opponents would call the extreme parties decided to have a discussion to see whether they could unite their forces and take a leaf out of the book of the Russian Revolution.

3   Strike and mutinies

When the pressure of wartime legislation and regulations was removed, the pent-up energies of the workers sought relief for their grievances, and demands were being put forward even before the General Election. The National Union of Railwaymen, for example, demanded the 8-hour day and nationalisation of the railways. Churchill at that moment was Minister of Munitions and more close to the life, if not of the workshop, at any rate of industry and services, than at any later period. Churchill in a speech announced himself in favour of the nationalisation of railways. Furthermore, while he was not the minister finally responsible, there is no question that his attitude played a part in the tactics of the government, which were to grant the 8-hour day to railwaymen rather than have a paralysing strike before the year ended. Other strikes took place, as we shall see; and in nearly every industry an extensive programme of social demands was being formulated and put forward with an insistent pressure for satisfaction.

Meantime there was an army of some 5 million.[1] When the war was over the question arose of demobilisation, plans for which, and the treatment of the soldiers immediately following the war, caused not merely a spirit of unrest but a whole series of mutinies.[2] There were, it is reckoned, a hundred mutinies in the British Army, many of them very serious and described by Churchill 25 years later as "a convulsion of indiscipline".[3] Churchill knew about it because on January 10 he was put in charge of the War Office and made at the same time Minister for Air. The mutinies were met by the most extensive and immediate concessions, and at once the main demand of the soldiers that demobilisation should be on the principle of 'first in, first out' was conceded.

There seems no question that, together with these purely domestic affairs, the demands put forward by the mutineers showed that the British working class were not disposed to accept the snap verdict of the electorate as final and definite. The same spirit was shown in the ranks of the trade unions. The feeling was that, considerable gains though it had made, the Labour Party had not been given its due representation; and that the victory for 'the man who won the war' had been an electoral trick.

Consequently the year 1919, beginning with mutinies, was marked by a succession of strikes and threatened strikes and industrial crisis on a scale which was almost unexampled, as we shall see in the next chapter. The first sign after the mutinies of a new spirit in the working class was that, so far from giving the impression of people who had been soundly thrashed at the polls, there was organised a series of gigantic demonstrations and amongst them demonstrations in favour of the workers' republic of Russia and against the intervention in that country. Demands were put forward insistently for the withdrawal of British troops from Murmansk, Archangelsk and elsewhere. These demands were channelled into a definite organisation, the Hands off Russia Committee. Many meetings were held, and throughout the country there was a steadily mounting agitation both for the withdrawal of the troops and for the cessation of the plans of intervention.

4   First move towards a revolutionary socialist party

The twelvemonth since November 7, 1917, had seen remarkable developments to which no great publicity was given at the time.

Events in Russia had given impetus to moves toward unity of the socialist parties and groupings in Britain. Already in April 1916 the United Socialist Council had been formed, being a joint committee of the Independent Labour Party and the British Socialist Party. It began its activities in 1917 and consisted, from the ILP, of four MPs, Macdonald, Snowden, Jowett and Anderson; from the BSP, Messrs H Alexander, E C Fairchild, A A Watts and Fred Shaw. A number of meetings were held but the matter had been jogging along rather slowly until the impact of the Russian Revolution.

The anti-war activity of the older socialist parties had gone on apace together with support for the Russian Revolution – mitigated in the case of the ILP by the growing pacifist influence within its ranks. But meanwhile in the workshops of Britain opposition to the war was growing, partly due to the increasingly harsh conditions which were making Britain into a 'labour prison', partly to the spreading disbelief in the aims of the Allies of the Entente. The Fourteen Points of President Wilson, however widely disseminated and however much they succeeded in reconciling Left-wing Liberals to a further support of the war, did not cut any ice in the workshops. There, all the circumstances above mentioned, combined with the appalling slaughter of the Somme battles ending in the suffocations of Paschendaele, had brought into many a home the most vehement feelings of revulsion to the war which so many had supported at its outset. The famous poem was being frequently repeated:

"I gave my life for freedom, this I know,
For those who bade me fight had told me so."

The combined result of all these things was what the government called "industrial unrest". Strike after strike broke out despite all repressions. The government and its supporters were uneasily aware that, however much they might imprison William Gallacher in 1916, or John Maclean in 1916 and 1918, there was no longer any possibility of its being believed, even by itself, that it was all due to 'pro-German agitators'. Robert Blatchford, the jingo editor of *The Clarion*, might write about the "Blatant Beast" in *John Bull* (a sensational weekly journal belonging to the well-known scoundrel, swindler and thief Horatio Bottomley) and discover that this character in Spenser's *Faerie Queene* was no other than the chairman of the Clyde Workers' Committee, William Gallacher. But all the revilings did not halt the spread and increasing militancy of the shop stewards' movement. Many of those shop stewards on the Clyde, in Yorkshire and elsewhere were members of the small Socialist Labour Party, the De Leonite organisation. As the war progressed some of them realised the need for unity of the working-class parties and that leadership by a single revolutionary party was more important than strict adherence to the tenets of Daniel De Leon.[4] A number of shop stewards, such as Tom Bell, Arthur MacManus, J T Murphy of Sheffield, with their theoretician William Paul, began to consider the possibility of joining up with other socialist parties. It proved impossible, however, to convince the main body of the SLP of this. The majority repudiated those members who were prominent shop stewards and retired into their 'Wee Free'[5] exclusiveness from which they have never since emerged.

Now, after the Revolution, and during the period when shop steward members of the SLP had gained a certain ascendancy, it was possible in December 1918 to hold a joint meeting of two of the constituents of the International Socialist Bureau[6] with MacManus, Bell and Murphy representing the Executive Council of the Socialist Labour Party. The proposal was to form a single revolutionary socialist party in Britain which would be able not only to welcome the Russian Revolution, but to carry on a struggle for revolutionary socialism in Britain and the British Empire. The representatives of the ILP were Fred Jowett and Philip Snowden, together with Francis Johnson. Unfortunately W C Anderson MP was fatally ill with Spanish influenza from which he died that winter.

No agreement was reached. The history of unsuccessful trade union attempts at amalgamation was repeated to some extent in this socialist attempt at unity. Before any agreement could be wrecked on the reef of finance the question of organisation came up as an insuperable barrier. The Socialist Labour Party delegate proposed that the new body should be based on workshop branches. To this the BSP put forward the strongest objections, and by all accounts it was on this preliminary reef that the vessel of unity was wrecked. It was a chance, but the chance was missed.

As soon as Ramsay Macdonald and Philip Snowden recovered their ascendancy within the ILP, the possibility of that body linking up with those who professed a Marxist basis was seen to be out of the question; in 1919 they were gradually able to wean their leading members away from such a venture. But in the meantime, however, other bodies outside the old International Socialist Bureau and outside its British Section had been developing, and others could be brought in. At the end of 1915 there had been formed the National Guilds League. Its guild socialist propaganda had been steadily developed in the columns of the weekly *Herald* by G D H Cole and William Mellor, the latter of whom in most cases actually wrote the articles. These arguments were also carried in the columns of the *Labour Leader* by Jack Cade.[7]

The Russian Socialist Revolution was saluted by the National Guilds League at its annual conference in 1918. But it was not until two years had passed that there began to develop a revolutionary wing amongst the national guildsmen which included not a few shop stewards.

In the East End of London there had been continued into the war the Women's Suffrage Federation headed by Sylvia Pankhurst. This presently became the Women's Socialist Federation and then the Workers' Socialist Federation. It had a very considerable influence in the East End of London but the claims for its influence in the minefields were not always to be substantiated by events and final affiliations

Meanwhile, also, in South Wales there had been a development of the pre-war Marxian Clubs, which presently in 1919 formed themselves into the South Wales Socialist Society. Its formation and its name enabled it to be regarded as a factor in the creation of a revolutionary socialist party, a Communist Party. However, it was so unorganised, so amorphous and with so little of a distinctive outlook that it was not surprising that it should simply have disintegrated in the spring of 1920. Some of its members thereafter attached themselves to one or other of the existing organisations.

On all of these bodies the impact of the Russian Revolution was now to take an organised form. This arose from the creation in March 1919 of the Communist International, with which we deal in Chapter 9.

Notes and References

1   The total of the British Empire armies in November 1918 was 193,000 officers, 4,144,841 other ranks. The total casualties have been given as 46,000 officers, 960,000 other ranks. The overwhelming majority of these were from Britain.

2   See A Rothstein, *The Soldiers' Strikes of 1919*, Palgrave MacMillan, 1980 –*Ed*.

3   W S Churchill, *The Dawn of Liberation: War Speeches*, Cassell & Co, London, 1945, p 49 –*Ed*.

4   Indeed it was James Connolly who had similarly found it impossible to carry out his remarkable revolutionary activities and at the same time dot every i and cross every t that proceeded from the facile pen of Daniel De Leon

5   The term 'Wee Free' derives from the dispute when the Scottish Free Church joined with the United Presbyterians, and the intransigent Highland parishes, in a small minority, claimed (and in 1902 obtained from the House of Lords) the title to the property of the whole Kirk; whereupon they were generally known as 'Wee Frees'.

6   *ie* the BSP and the ILP –*Ed*.

7   The author used this *nom de plume* for articles he wrote in the *Labour Leader*.

6 Intervention – 1919

I Ducal blood runs cold

So far from withdrawing their soldiers the Allied Governments intensified the attack on the Russian Republic at the end of the world war. After the conclusion of hostilities by the armistice of November 11, 1918, munitions made for use against the German enemy were transferred to the East of Europe against the people of Russia. Not only so, but factual alliance was made with the German military forces in occupation of Western parts of Russia. They were instructed not to withdraw immediately to their own frontiers, as we have seen.

Thus from September 1918 the ring was drawn more tightly round the Russian Soviet Federative Socialist Republic. No news came from inside that ring of hostile armed forces; or if any came it was scanty and more unreliable than ever. Consequently, not even the statesmen responsible[1] knew what exactly was happening inside. The whole of the newspapers of Europe and North America were turned into a wonderful breeding ground for the bacilli that carry poisonous rumours. Soon people were being conditioned to believe anything whatever about the Russian people and about the Bolsheviks.

There were, however, many military communiqués from the war fronts against the Soviets – the Southern Front, the South-Western Front, and so, around the compass. These communiqués, which could always, by richness and fertility of invention, make up for any poverty of factual successes, came either from White Guard generals, from the local headquarters of the 14 Allied powers invading Russia, or from both. The communiqués of the Red Army, which that winter recruited great numbers so that it grew from a few hundred thousand to a million men, were suppressed altogether or published only in a garbled form.

It had been assumed that the civil war, stimulated and sustained by the Allies, would speedily end in the extinction of Bolshevism; but it was not to be so. On the other hand there were those who hoped that the Peace Conference to be held at Paris in January in the New Year would also bring peace in Russia. Actually the question did come up, raised by Lloyd George. Neither he nor President Woodrow Wilson was so wholeheartedly bent on carrying intervention to its logical conclusion as some of their fellow statesmen. These two, while preparing for intervention, seemed willing to temporise. Wilson sent one agent to Stockholm and another agent to Moscow, and adopted a British proposal for a meeting of all parties on Prinkipo Island in the Sea of Marmora.[2]

Twenty years later Lloyd George claimed that he had tried to stop British intervention, but in vain. He says:

> "There were powerful and exceedingly pertinacious influences in the Cabinet working for military intervention in Russia, and as I was not on the spot in

London to exercise direct influence and control over the situation, for a while I was out-manoeuvred, and Mr Bonar Law, who presided over the Ministers in my absence, was overridden. Mr Winston Churchill in particular threw the whole of his dynamic energy and genius into organising an armed intervention against the Russian Bolshevik power."[3]

In another passage Lloyd George wrote that:

"the most formidable and irrepressible protagonist of an anti-Bolshevik war was Mr Winston Churchill. He had no doubt a genuine distaste for Communism. He was horrified, as we all were, at the savage murder of the Czar, the Czarina and their helpless children. His ducal blood revolted against the wholesale elimination of Grand Dukes in Russia."[4]

The Prinkipo proposal fell to the ground. The favourable communiqués of the anti-Soviet expeditions stifled any possibility of a similar proposal from the Allies. From this time on, intervention by the 14 capitalist countries grew. In the south, General Krasnov and General Dutov headed the Cossacks of the Don and the Caspian; while the armies of General Denikin, operating in conjunction with French, Greek and Rumanian detachments on the line of the Dniester, had pushed up from Odessa in a wide fan of which the eastward tip subtended the lower Volga. From beyond the Arctic Circle the British had moved from Archangelsk down the Northern Dvina until it seemed possible that their advance, together with the British warships on the Baltic and the activities of the Finns, would succeed in 'setting free' northern and north-eastern Russia from the revolutionary Russians. In the east Admiral Kolchak, who gave himself, and was accorded by the Allies, the title of "Supreme Ruler", gathered together counter-revolutionary forces and began a westward drive towards the Urals and towards Moscow. Finally, when this star in the east seemed to be nearing its zenith the Allied and associated powers (Britain, France, Italy, Japan and United States) promised all support and assistance; and sent him a dispatch which had an item demanding his acceptance of the burden of the "national debt". Kolchak in his reply (June 4, 1919) formally "accepted the burden of the National Debt of Russia"; in so doing he was giving an unmistakable sign of his adherence to the old regime. Even the dissolved Duma of 1906, in its Viborg Manifesto drawn up by the Cadet Party, had announced that they would not accept the responsibility of paying the interest on the bonds of the Russian loan floated on the British Stock Exchange and the Paris Bourse, which had given Tsardom a new lease of life. Kolchak's "acceptance of the burden" would have at once marked him out as a Tsarist had this not already been made manifest by his other actions. The dispatch, which was dated May 26, 1919, began in these words: "First, as soon as the Government of Admiral Kolchak and his Associates reach Moscow ...."

But the Red Armies had begun their drive eastward for a thousand miles and more, a drive which ended at Irkutsk with the mutiny of Kolchak's army.

2   Labour difficulties

What were the "labour difficulties" in Britain which hauled the Prime Minister out of the post-Armistice deliberations at Paris in the first weeks of 1919? They were difficulties for the British government raised by the mounting revolutionary spirit in the British working class.

The Lloyd George coalition government which had been returned with such an overwhelming majority on December 14, 1918, had hardly crossed the threshold of the New Year before it was encompassed with difficulties both at home and abroad. Abroad, the difficulties were above all those of Ireland, India and Egypt. At home the new spirit showed itself in a growing militancy within the trade unions. Trade unionists in Britain had numbered 4 million before the First World War but by 1920 there were some 8 million.

Issues which deeply stirred the organised labour movement included the attempt at violent suppression of the Irish struggle for independence. There was the use of auxiliary forces, the infamous Black-and-Tans, precursors and models for the shock troops of Hitler and the Nazis 15 years later.

They were also deeply stirred by the attempt to destroy 'the first workers' republic'. On March 26, 1919, the Miners' Federation of Great Britain had before it the Executive resolution which began with the words:

> "That this conference calls upon the Government to immediately withdraw all British troops from Russia, and to take the necessary steps to induce the Allied Powers to do likewise."[5]

In moving this resolution Herbert Smith of the Yorkshire Miners' Association (which had taken the initiative) said:

> "I want to submit to this conference that if we had no capitalistic money invested in Russia we should have no troops in Russia …. It is a betrayal of the lads who have been called up to take on military service in that direction. They ought to manage their own affairs; they ought to be left alone, and it is not for us to interfere and land troops there to protect capitalist interests."

James Winstone, vice-president of the South Wales Miners' Federation, seconding it, said:

> "This Government of ours are controlling the Press of this country, and not

allowing the truth about Russia to come out; if they did, possibly there would be almost, if not quite, a revolution against the treatment that has been meted out to the men who have been fighting for liberty, and for justice, and democracy. I think it is one of the greatest scandals, and one of the greatest reflections upon what we sometimes call this free British country of ours, that our troops should be sent there in order to prevent these men and these women, who like ourselves, are endeavouring to work out their own social salvation."

A leaflet written by Lenin had been distributed to the troops at Archangelsk. Clearly it came from men who held a not dissimilar outlook to that voiced by the speaker of the South Wales Miners' Federation.

The resolution was carried unanimously. Thereafter it was adopted by the combined ranks of the Miners' Federation of Great Britain, the National Union of Railwaymen and the Transport Workers' Federation, the Triple Industrial Alliance. It was adopted on April 16, 1919, and the pressure they exerted was soon to reach the point where it was made clear to the Prime Minister that unless Churchill and the war party were thwarted there would be a possibility of a General Strike of the whole Triple Industrial Advance and possibly of other sections as well. It was at this point that not only Lloyd George but the Cabinet as a whole capitulated and announced that intervention troops would be withdrawn. This was not to prevent Winston Churchill as War Minister and chief warmonger from striving to send further reinforcements to Archangelsk on the pretext that they would be required to assist the withdrawal.

3 Hands off Russia

The more general aspect of the resistance now growing up was voiced in the Hands off Russia movement very early in 1919. The London Hands off Russia committee was formed in January 1919. In the succeeding 6 months committees were formed in many places; and in September 1919 a central coordinating body was formed to give a lead in the agitation throughout the country against intervention in Russia. This was called the Hands off Russia National Committee. It focused attention on the question and affected all of the trade unions and to some extent the Co-operative movement as well. It included some of the most prominent and influential members of the trade unions and also of the Labour Party. It organised meetings and conferences. It supplied speakers to other organisations and issued leaflets and pamphlets. Under its stimulus innumerable trade union branches began to send in resolutions of protest against the government's Russian policy to Members of Parliament and to the Prime Minister. At the same time the pressure upon the Parliamentary Committee of the Trades Union Congress, already being exercised by the Triple Industrial Alliance, was intensified. On April 3, 1919, a joint conference of the Trades Union Congress and Labour Party was held in London, at which the following resolution, proposed by the Yorkshire Miners' association, was endorsed:

> "That this conference calls on the Government to take immediate steps to withdraw all British troops from Russia."[5]

The agitation went on and the capitalist press were compelled to give some expression to it. For example Vernon Hartshorn MP, arguing in defence of the Triple Alliance and the threatened Triple Alliance strike, wrote in the *Observer* on June 8, 1919:

> "The British workers see nothing in the attack on Russia but an effort on the part of a capitalistic Government to abuse the powers which have come to them through an election on quite another issue, to destroy a community based on Socialism."

The Labour Party conference which met on June 25-27, 1919, in Southport, showed a very different split from the Annual Conference a year earlier which had listened to Alexander Kerensky denouncing the Bolsheviks. Jack McGurk, the Lancashire miner who was in the chair, said in his presidential address:

> "We must resist military operations in Russia and perpetuation of conscription at home. There can be no peace so long as we continue to indulge in military adventures in Russia. ... It is useless for Mr Churchill to say we are not at war with Russia, and that we are only seeking to withdraw our troops already there, and at the same time for this country to take sides in the internal struggles that are presently going on in that country by sending men, munitions and materials to assist Admiral Kolchak to overcome the Bolshevist Revolution."[6]

4   The spirit of revolution

Meantime activity amongst the workers in Britain was rapidly increasing. A revolutionary spirit was spreading. It turned out that the January mutinies in the British Army were not only the product of specific grievances but of a general spirit of revolt. The witness is Lloyd George, who in a confidential memorandum of March 1919, to the Paris Peace Conference, said that the whole of Europe was "filled with the spirit of revolution".[7] He wrote that:

> "there is a deep sense not only of discontent, but of anger and revolt, amongst the workmen against the war conditions. The whole existing order in its political,

social and economic aspects is questioned by the masses of the population from one end of Europe to the other."

This was certainly true; and one side of it was the growing sharpness of the antagonism between the mass of the people and their governments precisely on the question of the attempt to crush the new socialist republic. On January 18 there was a London Workers' Committee meeting against intervention in Russia, whilst at the same time in Belfast, on January 27, there was a general strike. A general strike in Scotland, beginning on the Clyde at the end of that month – 'The Forty Hours Strike' – received support also from parts of England. The Riot Act was read in George Square, Glasgow, where William Gallacher, Emanuel Shinwell and others were arrested. By February 8 the British Socialist Party had organised a great Hands off Russia meeting in the Albert Hall. The Belfast strike came to an end after 3 weeks, but was immediately followed by threats of industrial action on a wider scale at a meeting of the Triple Industrial Alliance on February 25. This on the one hand caused the government to convene a 'national industrial conference', and on the other to take the most drastic steps to try to prevent a coalminers' strike by conceding a Royal Commission on the coalmining industry (the Sankey Commission), half of whose members were appointed by the Miners' Federation. It met on March 3. It was not until the Coal Commission had reported on March 20, and there had been a national conference of miners' delegates, that a strike of a million miners was postponed.

Nor was the unrest confined to the United Kingdom. In Canada there were severe struggles in Winnipeg, which lasted from March until June 1919, and included a general strike.[8] In India during April a demonstration had been repressed by British troops with much loss of life – the appalling Amritsar Massacre.[9] Meantime on the continent of Europe governments were formed following the model of Moscow. A Bavarian Soviet Government was set up, followed on March 23 by a Hungarian Soviet Government under the leadership of Bela Kun.

5. The *Daily Herald*

At this stage an immense part began to be played by the *Daily Herald* which after 4½ years reappeared on March 31. The effect of this new *Daily Herald* was very great throughout the working class. It was edited by George Lansbury and written by a staff of well-known journalists such as William Mellor (industrial editor), W N Ewer (foreign editor), W M Holmes and several other outstanding writers. All who were opposed to the government outside the regulation political parties were ready and willing to write for it. If the *Daily Herald* did not become the best collective agitator, organiser and propagandist or revolutionary spirit in Britain that spring of 1919, it was the nearest thing to it that had ever been seen in this country. In particular the *Daily Herald* was able to print news from Russia which was garbled or suppressed in the usual papers both of Fleet Street and throughout the country. It defended the new Soviet Republic. It played a yeoman part in destroying the barrage of lies about the military situation.

It had become the custom, as a hangover from wartime, for the military to stuff the papers with prognostications of how soon they would have a complete and overwhelming victory; and to back this up, even before action commenced, by communiqués of the most favourable nature. The *Daily Herald*, however, printed the communiqués of the Red Army which made no extravagant claims and were seen to be more truthful than those of White Guard generals.

Most of the staff at the *Daily Herald* were members of one or another socialist organisation, including some that had sprung up during the war itself, such as the National Guilds League and the Workers' Socialist Federation. But it should not be thought that it was either the organ of any party or had a definite attitude worked out beforehand on every question. It might be said there were all sorts in the *Daily Herald*. It had been powerfully backed by adherents of women's suffrage, of Sinn Fein, of Egyptian independence and of Indian independence, of pacifism and of many other special interests. Therefore it would be difficult to define it as other than a semi-revolutionary paper. The effect that it had in spreading ideas of socialism and fostering the spirit not only of discontent but of revolution and of class struggle should never be underestimated. In its news from outside Britain it was able to publish information about a series of happenings which otherwise would have been represented in a garbled or muted form. Consequently, for the first time, as it were, the curtain went up on the world outside Britain; and the real intensity of the class struggle and of the national liberation struggle in country after country was revealed.

For example, it was possible after the report of an unusually effective May Day demonstration in London and many of the great towns, as well as in places where May Day had never been celebrated before, to tell, in addition to the Red Army communiqués, of the struggle inside the British Empire. There was on June 1 in Hyde Park a demonstration of police and prison officers; in the first weeks of June 1919 there were great widespread strikes in France. By the end of that week the strikes in Canada were spreading and from France they were reaching beyond into Belgium and Italy.

Notes and References

1   Statement of Lloyd George at the Paris Peace Conference discussion on the Russian issue beginning January 16, 1919:
    "(a) We did not know the facts about Russia. Differing reports were received from our representatives in Russia, and often reports from the same representative varied from day to day. It was clear that, unless we knew the facts. we should not be in a position to form a correct judgment.
    "(b) On one subject there could certainly be complete agreement, to wit, that the condition of Russia was extremely bad.

There was anarchy and starvation, and all the suffering resulting from both. It was impossible to know which party was gaining the upper hand, but hopes that the Bolshevik Government would collapse had certainly been disappointed.

Bolshevism appeared to be stronger than ever. Mr. Lloyd George quoted a report from the British Military Authorities in Russia, who could not be suspected of leanings towards Bolshevism, to the effect that the Bolshevik Government was stronger now than it had been some months previously. The peasants feared that all other parties would, if successful, restore the ancient regime and deprive them of the land which the Revolution had put into their hands."

(D Lloyd George, *The Truth about the Peace Treaties*, Vol 1, Victor Gollancz, London, 1938, p. 332)

2   See Appendix I to this chapter.

3   Lloyd George, *op cit*, p 367.

4   *Ibid*, pp 324-5.

5   This and the following two quotations are taken from R Page Arnot, *The Miners: Years of Struggle*, George Allen & Unwin, London, 1953, p 227 –*Ed*.

6   Quoted, eg, in W P and Z Coates, *A History of Anglo-Soviet Relations*, Lawrence & Wishart, 1943, p 143 – *Ed*.

7   Quoted, eg, in E H Carr, *A History of Soviet Russia Vol 3: The Bolshevik Revolution* (1917-1923), Norton Paperback Editions, New York, 1985 (Macmillan, 1953), p 128 –*Ed*.

8   See Appendix II to this chapter.

9   See Appendix III to this chapter.

Appendix I

At the Paris Peace Conference

A discussion at the Paris Peace Conference "on the Russian issue" took place on January 21, 1919. Before the discussion concluded and after two ambassadors had been heard giving evidence, President Woodrow Wilson read a very remarkable message he had just received from his agent W H Buckler at Stockholm as to confidential conversations with Litvinov. This message indicated that the Soviet Government was anxious to negotiate.

> "Litvinov stated that the Soviet Government are anxious for a permanent peace, and fully endorse the telegram which he sent to President Wilson, the December 24. They detest the military preparations and costly campaigns which are now forced upon Russia after four years of exhausting war, and wish to ascertain whether the United States and the Allies have a desire for peace.
>
> "If such is the case, peace can easily be negotiated, for, according to Litvinov, the Soviet Government are prepared to compromise on all points, including protection to existing foreign enterprises, the granting of new concessions in Russia, and the Russian foreign debt. It is impossible now to give the details as to possible compromises, because Litvinov has no idea of the claims which will be presented by the Allies, nor of the resources which will be available to Russia for the satisfaction of those claims .... The Soviet Government's conciliatory attitude is unquestionable.
>
> "Litvinov showed me an open wireless message which he had just received from Chicherine, the Soviet Foreign Minister, affirming the willingness of the Government to be conciliatory with reference to the question of the foreign debt. Litvinov and his associates realise fully that Russia will need, for a long time, expert assistance and advice, particularly in financial and technical matters, and that she cannot get on without manufactured imports, including, especially, foreign machinery."[1]

On the evening of January 21, 1919, Lloyd George brought the matter up before the British Empire delegation so as to ensure unanimity of support for any policy he might present to the Peace Conference. But the Prime Ministers of the Empire, "when they had contemplated this terrible portent in Eastern Europe", took a decision which the minute reveals to have been uncommonly ambiguous:

> "It was agreed:
> "(1) that the Prime Minister and the Secretary of State for Foreign Affairs

should make it clear at the conversations that we could not agree to a continuance of intervention in Russia, or of subsidies to the forces of the other Allies engaged in operations with this object. If, however, some effort could be made to bring the contending parties in Russia together, which the British Empire Plenipotentiaries could regard as satisfactory such as summoning the various parties to meet, for example, at Salonica or Lemnos, the withdrawal of the British Empire forces at present in Russia would not be immediate.

"(2) That as regards any steps which the Great Powers might think it necessary to take in order to protect against invasion of any independent State about to be set up, we should be ready to co-operate."[2]

On the next day, January 22, President Wilson tabled his draft which was adopted "to be publicly transmitted to the parties invited". The usual remarks disclaiming any intention "to interfere in any manner" in Russia whose people "they regarded as their friends, not their enemies" (even saying that "they recognise the absolute right of the Russian people to direct their own affairs" and that "they recognise the Revolution without reservation, and will in no way, and in no circumstances, aid or give countenance at any attempt at a counter-revolution") were all preliminary to the actual proposal which ran:

"They invite every organised group that is now exercising, or attempting to exercise, political authority or military control anywhere in Siberia, or within the boundaries of European Russia as they stood before the war just concluded (except in Finland) to send representatives, not exceeding three representatives for each group, to the Princes Islands, Sea of Marmora, where they will be met by representatives of the associated powers, provided, in the meantime, there is a truce of arms amongst the parties invited".[3]

After a reference to "the fourteen articles upon which the present negotiations are based" the object of this rendezvous at Prinkipo was said to be "some understanding and agreement by which Russia may work out her own purposes and happy co-operative relations be established between her people and the other peoples of the world."

A prompt reply was requested, and a date set:

"The representatives will be expected at the place appointed by February 15, 1919."

The communiqué containing the proclamation was wirelessed after 9 pm on

January 22. The Bolsheviks however never received the official invitation – the wireless was jammed by the French Government – but they did learn of it and on February 4, 1919, they sent a reply accepting. They never heard of it again.

President Wilson meantime had sent an envoy to Russia, William C Bullitt, a young State Department official attached to the US Peace Delegation – who was accompanied by the well-known American journalist Lincoln Steffens who became famous for his 8-word declaration:

"I have seen the future: and it works."[4]

But the talk about negotiations came to nothing.

Notes and references

1   See Office of the Historian, Department of State, United States of America, *Papers Relating To The Foreign Relations Of The United States, The Paris Peace Conference, 1919*, Volume III, Paris Peace Conf 180.03101/11, BC–6, Annex "A" to IC–113 [BC–6], online at https://history.state.gov/historicaldocuments/frus1919Parisv03/d38 –*Ed.*
2   Lloyd George, *op cit*, p 353.
3   *Ibid*, p 365f.
4   Repeated. in these words, by Steffens to the author in Spring 1919.

Appendix II

A General Strike in Winnipeg, Canada

The long general strike in Winnipeg in 1919 showed signs of taking on a revolutionary character. There had been growing activity and influence in Western Canada of the 'One Big Union' movement which stood for the reorganising of the existing 'international' craft unions affiliated to the American Federation of Labor into one compact industrial organisation of workers divided into sections by industry. On March 14, 1919, at the Calgary Western Labour Convention, the Canadian Western Labour Unions finally adopted this scheme by an overwhelming majority, together with an advanced programme including the demand for a 30-hour week. On April 9 the government appointed a Royal Commission. On May 1 the unrest came to a head with strikes in the metal trades at Toronto and in the metal and building trades at Winnipeg.

On May 15 the Winnipeg strike became general. The whole body of 30,000 workers came out and a long drawn-out struggle followed between the Citizens' Committee of One Thousand, representing the employers and professional classes, and the Strike Committee. At the beginning the Strike Committee had complete control of the city, took charge of the supply services, maintained order and prevented the appearance of the non-labour press. During that period no disorder was reported; it was not until a month later, when the Citizens' Committee had broken the complete control of the Strike Committee by their volunteer defence force, and after Government action, that disturbances began. A feature of the strike was the wholehearted support of the majority of the returned soldiers. Sympathetic movements took place in most of the cities of Western Canada. On June 7 the Canadian Government rushed through an amendment to their Immigration Act, giving power to deport British-born subjects equally with aliens. On June 17 they proceeded to arrest the 10 principal strike leaders at Winnipeg. The strike ended on June 25.

Appendix III

The Amritsar Massacre

In the second week of April in 1919, in India, the Amritsar Massacre took place. The Amritsar atrocity, the shooting down and massacring of a helpless and unarmed crowd of Hindu men, women and children assembled in an orderly meeting (for which a prohibition order had been served), was carried through by General Dyer. A total of 379 peaceful people were killed outright; 1,200 wounded were left lying there bleeding without means of attention. The Amritsar Massacre made it certain that only a few years would pass before the British were out of India and the country proclaimed a Republic. Those then leading the Indian people would not see death before they saw the republic of their desire. At the time the news of this April atrocity in Amritsar in the Punjab was officially suppressed; it was not until 8 months had gone by that Parliament and the British public were informed. General Dyer, however, the "hero" of this infamy, so far from receiving "immediate drastic punishment" was given a purse of £20,000 and obtained a vote of approval from the House of Lords.

7 Intervention – 1920

1 Autumn 1919

On September 30, 1919, the Supreme Council of the victorious powers at Versailles decided to maintain a "peaceful blockade" of Russia. Notes were sent to the neutral governments and to the vanquished German Government with the request that "all nations which desire peace and the re-establishment of the social order should unite together to resist the Bolshevik Government". The call was made for a complete prohibition of all trade, communications of persons, credits or postal intercourse between other countries and Bolshevik Russia. These Notes were not made public in this country nor in the French Republic and only became known later through the publication of the Note to the German Government in the German press.

By November 1919 the Blockade Note proposing a universal blockade of Russia had been answered by the countries to whom it was addressed. Germany and Italy both declined to take part. Cecil Harmsworth, a junior member of the government, declared that in view of the German refusal it was not certain whether the blockade would be enforced. The policy of 'intercepting' ships to Russia by British Naval forces in the Baltic was stated by the British Government not to be a blockade in the technical sense. Why? Because technically, though war was being conducted, Britain was not in a state of war with Russia.

At this point, while pressure was being maintained as far as possible by the workers in Britain and in other countries, there came the sudden announcement by Lloyd George that it was impossible to continue effectively with the intervention in the Soviet Union and that "the last British troops sailed for home from Murmansk on October 12, 1919, and from Vladivostock on November 1, 1919". On November 8 however there was still a British military mission with the counter-revolutionary forces in southern Russia. These, as well as all other anti-Soviet forces from Murmansk to Constantinople, continued to receive enormous quantities of munitions and supplies.

On November 8 Lloyd George in a speech at the Guildhall said that Britain had sent "£100 million-worth of material and of support in every form" to the counter-revolutionary generals, and then added:

> "We cannot, of course, afford to continue so costly an intervention in an interminable civil war. Our troops are out of Russia. Frankly I am glad. Russia is a quicksand. Victories are easily won in Russia, but you sink in victories; and great armies and great Empires in the past have been overwhelmed in the sands of barren victories.
>
> "Russia is a dangerous land to intervene in. We discovered it in the Crimea. But true to the instinct which has always saved us we never went far from the sea, and we were able to extricate ourselves from there."[1]

The Tory newspapers furiously attacked Lloyd George. The joint council of the Trades Union Congress and the Labour Party, however, at once resolved that

> "[It] welcomes the Prime Minister's statement at the Guildhall, indicating that the British Government would immediately bring to an end the support now being given to the warfare now being carried on in different parts of Russia, and seek the means of bringing about peace in that country".

The joint meeting further urged that:

> "steps should be taken at once to withdraw all British forces from any warlike enterprises in or about the territories formerly included in the Russian Empire; and to stop all further supplies of stores, munitions or tanks".[2]

2 Interventionist skirmishes

As the forces of British infantry and other arms were about to be withdrawn from Archangelsk and Murmansk and Vladivostok, the activities of the British Navy were stimulated by the anti-Bolshevik section of the government. On August 18 there was a British Naval attack on the Russian Fleet. On the other hand, new defenders of Soviet Russia stood up. Prof W T Goode (author of *Bolshevism at Work*) was one of those who, unconnected hitherto with the Labour movement, simply by becoming acquainted with conditions in Russia had been overcome by a feeling of revulsion at the behaviour of the government. Another was Lt-Col Malone MP, elected in 1918 as Coalition Liberal, who, having been to the Soviet Union, was able to tell the truth. On September 6, 1919, Lt-Col Sherwood Kelly VC denounced the war against the Soviet Union. Lastly there was Captain Harold Grenfell, former British Naval Attaché at Petrograd, who had realised that the fate of mankind was at stake; outstanding amongst all his fellow diplomats and attachés, he had boldly taken the side of the Soviets. These men were willing to speak at meetings: the largest halls were filled by enthusiastic audiences to hear them not only in London but in the main towns of Great Britain.

In that same month of October 1919 there was, on October 5, the settlement of the national railway strike which had stirred up the class consciousness of all workers. But the other side had also been active. On October 7 the Prime Minister announced that counter-strike preparations had been made ever since February 1919. Indeed on October 3 the civic guard had been set up by the government. From abroad the news came on October 13 that a drive northward had resulted in the capture by General Denikin of Orel, and that on October 16 Kronstadt, the fortress on the Gulf of Finland just outside Petrograd, had "surrendered under bombardment of the British Navy". The Navy was very active. This stimulated a great demonstration in the Albert Hall organised by the *Daily Herald* on two issues: "Peace with Russia and Nationalisation of the Mines". This was an example of the way in which the immediate domestic demands in industry of the workers were now being linked up with the defence of the Soviet Union and the insistence on ending the war against her.

3 A special Trades Union Congress

Following on the resolution passed by the Trades Union Congress at Glasgow in the first week of September 1919, a special Congress to hear the report of the deputation from the Parliamentary Committee to the Prime Minister had been summoned for December 9 and 10. Displeased with the Prime Minister's reply, the special TUC passed the following resolution:

> "That this Congress having heard the report of the deputation which waited upon the Prime Minister on the question of Russia, expresses its profound dissatisfaction; it calls upon the Government immediately to consider the peace overtures made by the Soviet Government; and, further, to raise the blockade and allow facilities for trade between Russia and the outside world. Congress demands the right of independent and impartial enquiry into the industrial, political and economic conditions of Russia and instructs the Parliamentary Committee to appoint a delegation to visit Russia and to demand passport facilities from the Government for this purpose, and that a further report of Russia be considered at our next special Trades Union Congress."

Only that week there had arrived in London the eleventh Russian peace offer. In less than 18 months Chicherin had sent nearly a dozen deliberate, solemn and carefully worded peace offers, all of which had been completely ignored.

Meantime, however, the fortunes of Churchill's foreign protegés were no longer so happy. In December the Red Army was able to inflict defeat after defeat upon Denikin. Kharkov on December 11 was captured by the Red Army; Kiev, capital of the Ukraine, on December 17. On December 30 a revolution took place in Irkutsk, which had become Kolchak's capital after he had abandoned Omsk on October 30. On January 15 Kolchak fled and sought Allied protection. The next day Denikin's army surrendered at Mariupol. By the 9th Rostov-on-Don had been captured by the Red Army.

The Supreme Council of the Allies decided on January 16 to begin trade with Russia through the Russian Co-operative organisations. Background to these decisions was, on the one hand, the military situation in Russia, and on the other, the growing pressure in the United Kingdom.

4 The blockade raised

On January 12, 1920, the Supreme Council announced the raising of the blockade on Germany. On the 16th it announced that, with a view to relieving distress in the interior of Russia, where there was famine, facilities would be granted to the Russian Co-operative organisations to "arrange for the import into Russia of clothing, medicines, agricultural machinery and the other necessaries of which the Russian people are in sore need, in exchange for grain, flax etc, of which Russia has surplus supplies".[3] These arrangements so far implied no change in policy of the Allied Governments towards the Soviet Government.

A breakthrough, however, became clear in the month of January 1920. The Hands off Russia National Committee once more circularised all trade union branches pointing out that nothing but industrial action would force the hand of the government. It organised big demonstrations. In the Albert Hall, London, on February 27, 1920, an audience packed to the doors, with Tom Mann in the chair, heard the speeches of Professor W T Goode, Col Malone MP, Israel Zangwill, Robert Williams, secretary of the International Transport Workers' Federation, and finally Captain Harold Grenfell. The account given in the *Daily Herald* said that Israel Zangwill, the well-known novelist, spoke of the failure of the Churchillian policy against Russia and said that the object of intervention in Russia "was to keep Bolshevism out of England. Has it done so?" Then, as the *Daily Herald* reported:

> "His glance swept over the crowded arena and round the loaded galleries, tier above tier, up to the twilight of the dome, and from every quarter came back full-throated the inevitable answer."

A couple of weeks later George Lansbury returned from a short visit to Russia. The *Daily Herald* announced that it had booked the Albert Hall for a meeting on the following Sunday, March 21. Every ticket was sold within two hours. Again Tom Mann was in the chair. Lansbury got a tremendous reception. One and all waited to hear from one of the favourite leaders of the Labour movement what he had found in Russia. Other speakers in past demonstrations had been worthy but unknown to the mass of the workers before they had taken their stand on behalf of Soviet Russia. But George Lansbury was bone of their bone and flesh of their flesh to the Londoners. He told what he had seen and what Lenin had said to him, in a speech which was like a heart-to-heart talk. Beside him on the platform was Jean Longuet, the grandson of Karl Marx. For many it seemed the culmination of two generations of socialism in Britain and the inauguration of an era of world socialism.

5 Trade with Russia

After the decision of the Supreme Council on January 16, 1920, to permit trade with Russia through the Co-operative organisations, the hoped for progress was slow. Delay was caused first by objections being raised to the inclusion of Soviet Commissars in the trade commission[4] appointed to represent the Russian Co-operative societies. Eventually on April 7, 1920, the Russian commission met the Inter-Allied representatives at Copenhagen. A further hitch then occurred through the demand of the Allies that the Soviet Government should first recognise the debts of the former Russian State, and guarantee compensation for confiscated foreign properties. This the Russian delegates pointed out was a question for negotiation with the Soviet Government and not with the Co-operative representatives.

Meanwhile steps for resumption of trade had been actually taken by other countries than Britain. A Russo-Italian Commercial Convention was signed on March 31 between Litvinov, on behalf of the Central Union of Russian Co-operatives, and Cabrini, on behalf of the National League of Italian Co-operatives. On March 7 the United States Government announced the lifting of the Russian trade embargo. Private negotiations with trading firms began to take place.

6 The Marquess Curzon at the Foreign Office

The Marquess Curzon, Leader of the House of Lords, from December 1916 onward one of the 5 original members of the War Cabinet in the coalition headed by Lloyd George, became Foreign Secretary on October 23, 1919. His interests were those of one who had been Viceroy of India from 1898 to 1905. His eyes were ever upon the Asian scene where the tradition of three generations regarded Russia, whatever its government, as a rival power. The Marquees Curzon at the outset of the tentative trade negotiations communicated with the Soviet Government to ask if it would grant an amnesty for the remnant of Denikin's army on the coast of the Black Sea. Under this amnesty the troops of Denikin were to be withdrawn by fleets under British control: actually there was a very considerable re-equipment and gathering of new forces which were put under the command of General Wrangel. Thus, at the very moment when it had seemed that peace would at last be achieved, a new war was to begin again from the south.

The defeat of the other Tsarist generals had been the signal for Marshal Pilsudski of Poland to begin on April 24 an invasion of Soviet Russia. The Polish armies drove toward the Ukraine, which apparently it was the intention to incorporate in the new Polish state. This invasion of the Ukraine coincided with a telegram sent on May 3 by King George V congratulating the Polish dictator on the first anniversary of the setting up of the Polish state. Three months later, August 16, 1920, Lord Robert Cecil was saying in the House of Commons, "Then there was the message which His Majesty was unfortunately advised to send to Marshal Pilsudski". On May 8 Kiev was captured by the Poles. At the very moment when the British Labour delegation was in Petrograd on May 12, and while the Russian Co-operative Trade delegation was expected in London, a new war was being launched on Soviet Russia.

7 The episode of the *Jolly George*

The extreme danger of a renewal of the war by the militarists of France, Poland, Britain and other Allied countries roused the working class of Britain. On May 10, 1920, the steamship *Jolly George* was being loaded in a London dock. The dockers noticed munitions among the cargoes consigned to Poland. They immediately ceased work; nor would they proceed with the loading of the remainder of the cargo nor with the bunkering of the steamer until the munitions were unloaded. All that afternoon of May 10 and the next day the cargo was untouched.

On May 12 it was reported there was enough cargo to make the trip worthwhile; and enough coal to take the *Jolly George* to Danzig. In any case she was fitted with sails and if need be could make the trip under canvas and would sail on May 13 as scheduled. This announcement did not dismay the dockers. They refused to continue loading. On the same day, May 12, the owners approached Fred Thompson, London District secretary of the dockers' union and agreed to the men's terms. The chairman of the company, J P Walford, stated:

> "The Walford Line rather than give any colour to the belief that they were doing other than acting quite bona fide, and in order that no occasion should be given for committing an industrial dispute, have given an instruction for the cargo of munitions to be discharged and the full cargo of general goods may be dispatched at the earliest possible moment.
> "The cargo already loaded will be discharged tomorrow morning and the trade unionists have promised that the work shall be expedited" *(Daily News, 13.v.1920)*

On the same day the *Daily Herald* had an interview with Fred Thompson who said:

> "I have received a number of resolutions from London branches of the union declaring in strong terms that their members would refuse to load war material for Poland or any other enemy of the Russian Republic. We shall keep our eyes open and see that the munitions are not surreptitiously put aboard any other ship." *(13.v.1920)*

Meantime others came into prominence. Credit is ascribed to Ernest Bevin by his biographer Alan Bullock for the official action he took as general secretary of the dockers' union. But it was Harry Pollitt, then a young boilermaker, who by his agitation among the dockers personified the workers' anger at the trickery of the government and the employers. Pollitt's dockside meetings led to the first decision to stop loading the *Jolly George*. Then Fred Thompson took up the men's case, and Bevin came in with his official action at the very end.

8 The war against Russia

The winter after the breakdown of the combined Denikin-Kolchak-Yudenich attempts had been occupied, as in the previous winter, with peace talk which engaged the attention of public opinion at home while extensive military preparations were being made for a spring offensive. On January 16, 1920, the Supreme Council of the Allies had announced its intention of raising the blockade and encouraging trade with Russia; and on February 24 it recommended the border states to make peace with Russia.

Meanwhile British warships were still bombarding the Black Sea ports; Britain, France and America combined to equip and supply the Polish Army; Clemenceau had openly declared in December 1919 the intention of exercising economic pressure on Poland and the border states to carry on war against Russia. Poland, whose statesmen were in constant communication with the Allies, refused, on what Lord Robert Cecil afterwards declared "seemingly flimsy pretexts", to entertain the "repeated and genuine offers of peace" of the Russian Soviet Government.

In April 1920, the new offensive had begun. It comprised the following:

(1) A Polish-Ukrainian combination (Pilsudski and Petliura) in the west and south-west;

(2) The remains of General Denikin's forces under General Wrangel in the south, supported by British warships ;

(3) A Japanese offensive in eastern Siberia.

On April 24 the Polish attack had been launched on a 250-mile front and reached Kiev on May 8.

Allied complicity was at first denied, and afterwards admitted. On May 6 Bonar Law denied that the government was giving moral or material support to Poland; yet on May 11 Winston Churchill admitted that the British and French Governments had "helped to strengthen and equip the Polish army."

9 Vicissitudes of 'Trade with Russia'

The Allies, meeting at San Remo on May 5, decided that their representatives should meet the Russian Trade Delegation (which must not include Litvinov) and negotiate for resumption of trade through the medium of Co-operative societies. Already in Russia a People's Commissariat for Foreign Trade had been set up. By the middle of May the Co-operative organisation had arrived in London, and with the arrival of Leonid Krassin, Commissar of Transport, negotiations began on May 31. A number of conferences took place between Krassin and the Prime Minister. After a month of these negotiations a breakdown appeared imminent: it was on the question of the restitution of Allied private property.

On June 29 Krassin handed to Lloyd George a Note in which, after a detailed statement of the difficulties which had been placed in the way of negotiations by the raising of purely political questions, without any proper facilities for communication with Moscow being allowed, and a further examination of the inadmissibility of peace conference claims being made conditions of commercial intercourse without a peace conference, he stated that should the British Government be unwilling to enter into official negotiations for the resumption of peace, immediate resumption of economic and commercial relations would, nevertheless, be possible on the following basis:

1. All questions of foreign policy or of mutually material claims of governments and subjects to be postponed to a peace conference.
2. The two governments to proclaim resumption as above.
3. The fundamental principles for resumption to be
    (a) removal of mines in the Baltic Sea etc;
    (b) complete freedom of navigation to and from Russian ports;
    (c) commercial relations on a basis of reciprocity and immunity;
    (d) validity of passports and other documents to be recognised.

Finally Krassin stated:

"In conclusion, on behalf of the Government of the Russian Socialist Federal Soviet Republic, I have the honour to bring under the notice of the British Government and the entire British people, and particularly the British labouring masses, that it is the most urgent and earnest wish of the Government of Soviet Russia and of the entire Russian peoples to conclude at the earliest possible date a full and general peace, without reservation, with all the Powers who in recent years have taken part in hostile acts against her."

On July 1 Krassin embarked on a British destroyer *en route* for Moscow with a reply from Lloyd George in which the following conditions were laid down:

1. No propaganda by either party, particularly not by the Soviet Government, amongst Asiatics against the interests of the British Empire.
2. Immediate repatriation of British and Russian subjects.
3. Each government to recognise liability for compensation to private citizens for goods and services rendered, determination of liabilities to be left to a peace conference.
4. The conditions as to commercial facilities etc, accepted.

To this on July 10 Georgy Chicherin replied from Moscow.

Chicherin accepted in his Note these conditions put by Lloyd George, but not without a protest against the "affirmation, contrary to the real facts, relative to the presumed attacks of Soviet Russia upon the British Empire".

On July 11, Lord Curzon replied from Spa[5], noting the acceptance and intimating that the negotiations would be resumed as soon as the delegates could return. To this was added a further proposal with regard to an armistice between Russia and Poland.

Meantime Kamenev and Milyutin were added to the Krassin delegation which set out from Reval at the mouth of the Gulf of Finland. In his Note to Chicherin of July 20, Lord Curzon intimated that the delegation must now delay their departure from Reval until the Russo-Polish Armistice had been agreed to. In his reply of July 24, dealt with below, Chicherin protested against this violation of the agreement. He stated that the establishment of durable relations would be rendered difficult if agreements, after being adopted, were to be supplemented by new and unexpected conditions not stipulated earlier.

10   Visissitudes of international politics

The Armistice Note from Lord Curzon of July 11 put forward a provisional Polish frontier: a line 30 kilometres east of this was not to be crossed by the Russian armies. A peace conference was to be held in London between Russia and all the border states. An armistice with General Wrangel was to be signed and the Isthmus of Perekop which leads to the Crimea was to become a neutral zone; while Wrangel himself was to be invited to London, but not as a member of the conference there. If, however, Soviet Russia intended to cross that provisional frontier into Polish territory the British Government and their Allies, invoking the Covenant of the League of Nations, would assist the Poles with all the means at their disposal. A week was given for a reply.

To this Note Chicherin replied on July 19 in a lengthy and extremely well-written Note. He expressed his pleasure at the new-found desire of the British Government for peace in Eastern Europe: while he pointed out that Britain, being still in a state of war with the Soviets, was not really qualified to act as mediator.

He referred to an error of fact, namely, that the head of the British Government had been unaware of the Russo-Georgian Treaty of Peace: furthermore that

> "the British Government was deprived of all information regarding the peace between Russia and Lithuania when, in its ultimatum of July 12, it had pointed to Lithuania as one of the border states with which Russia has still to obtain peace".

His other points were that Russia was prepared to make peace at once by direct negotiation with Poland. He offered Poland a better frontier than that proposed by the Allies. He offered to the "mutinous ex-General Wrangel" personal security for all his troops and all civilians in return for complete capitulation; but he declined the proposal of the London conference as unnecessary. Furthermore he declined to admit the right to interfere of the "group of governments called the League of Nations" from which the Russian Government had never received "any communication as to its creation and had never had the opportunity of adopting a decision as to the recognition or non-recognition of the association of states".

Lord Curzon's reply stated that the Polish Government was now being urged by the Allies to apply for an armistice. The reply was dated July 20. The Poles did so apply on July 23 and the Soviet Government thereupon directed its Supreme Command to make arrangements for an armistice.

On Saturday July 24 Chicherin sent a Note to Lord Curzon in which he intimated that orders had been given to the Russian Supreme Command to begin pourparlers with Poland for an armistice and a peace; and went on to propose that the peace conference of Russia and the leading powers of the Entente should be held in London. On Tuesday July 27 Lloyd George met the French Premier Millerand at Boulogne; there it was decided to agree to a general peace conference provided that Poland and all the border states took part; but if the Soviet Government made peace with Poland separately then the general coherence would be refused.

Notes and References

1   Quoted, eg, in W P and Z Coates, *A History of Anglo-Soviet Relations*, Lawrence & Wishart, 1943, p 2 –*Ed*.
2   Quoted, eg, in W P and Z Coates, *A History of Anglo-Soviet Relations*, Lawrence & Wishart, 1943, p 2 –*Ed*.
3   See Office of the Historian, Department of State, United States of America, *Papers Relating To The Foreign Relations Of The United States, The Paris Peace Conference, 1919*, Volume III, Paris Peace Conf 180.03101/5, ICP-18, Annex C to ICP-18, online at https://history.state.gov/historicaldocuments/frus1919Parisv09/d35 –*Ed*.
4   The commission consisted of Krassin, Litvinov. Rosovsky, Nogin and Khinchuk.
5   The Spa conference was the first post-WW1 conference to include German representatives.

8 British Parties and Councils of Action

I 'Hands off Russia' in Summer 1920

Growing anger in the Labour movement at the wanton Polish attack on Soviet Russia backed by Britain and France (and very spectacularly in the case of Britain by the despatch of George V's telegram) kept mounting during the month of May and throughout the summer. Throughout that month of May a stirring appeal from the Hands off Russia National Committee was being circulated throughout trade union branches, trades councils, Labour parties and branches of socialist parties, which ran as follows:

> "Russia is attacked solely because our class, the working class, is in power, and they have demonstrated that 'Labour is fit to govern'. Fellow trade unionists, don't allow this fearful crime to go on. Russia wants peace, the working classes of Poland want peace, the masses of Europe and of the world want peace. The inhuman imperialists and militarists want war. You can make the British Government give the word which will bring peace to suffering humanity in Eastern Europe.
>
> "Mere pious resolutions won't force the hands of the Government, but resolutions backed by industrial action will."

The industrial action that stopped the *Jolly George* on May 10 was one immediate example of this. Now there began to be more and more evidence of a growing demand for strike action. The miners were prominent. For example, a letter from the Durham Miners' Association, "protesting against the help given to the Poles by the British and Allied Governments" for their war on Russia, convinced the Executive Committee of the Miners' Federation of Great Britain, meeting on May 21, 1920, that they should send a strong protest to the Prime Minister. Ten days later the matter was taken up at a meeting of the Triple Alliance subcommittee, which "in view of the extreme urgency of the question" took on themselves the responsibility of pressing for a special Trades Union Congress to deal not only with the Polish war upon Russia but also the military operations in Ireland.

Three weeks later the Miners' Federation Executive Committee passed a resolution:

> "That the British Government in refusing to allow Ireland the form of Government chosen by the Irish people, and in assisting Poland in her attack on the Russian Republic, is betraying all the principles for which our nation fought, and that the most effective way in which a protest can be made is for the organised workers to refuse to manufacture or transport munitions of war for Ireland or Poland." *(9.vi.1920)*[1]

On June 10, the next day, the Miners' Federation of Great Britain Special Conference condemned the "ruthless attack" on the liberties and independence of the Irish people, demanded immediate withdrawal of the troops and urged the Parliamentary Committee to expedite the calling of a special Trades Union Congress "to determine the attitude of organised labour towards the production and handling of munitions of war for Ireland and Poland".[2]

A manifesto was published in the *Daily Herald* on May 22, 1920. It was signed, amongst others, by many trade union leaders.[3] It appealed to trade unionists throughout Britain "to demand that the Parliamentary Committee of the Trades Union Congress, and the Executive Committee of the Labour Party, should convene a national conference, without a moment's avoidable delay, in order to declare a national 'down-tools' policy of 24 hours to enforce peace with Russia". The Hands off Russia Committee appealed for money to enable it to print the maximum number of copies of this appeal. In the weeks that followed the appeal was distributed in hundreds of thousands of copies in working-class centres throughout the country.

Meantime the British Labour and Trade Union delegation returned from Russia early in 1920. Its interim report was concerned with and indeed was confined to the disastrous effects of the Allied policy of intervention and blockade.

The agitation throughout the month of June continued. While negotiations for peace and trade were going on in London the effect of both the Hands off Russia Committee appeals and of the interim report of the British Labour delegation were spreading throughout the working class.

The interim report of the TUC was signed by Ben Turner, F L (Ethel) Snowden, A A Purcell, H Skinner, Tom Shaw MP, Robert Williams and Margaret Bondfield; and a delegation from the ILP headed by R C Wallhead and Clifford Allen signifed their endorsement of the report. The report, which appeared in the press on June 12, 1920 (the day on which the Red Army recaptured Kiev from Polish forces, which they then began to drive back towards their own country and out of Soviet Russia) stated (p 28) "we have been profoundly impressed by the effects of the policy of intervention and blockade upon the Russian people". This policy "still being pursued today, was at the root of the worst evils afflicting Russia. Then it said:

> "The problem of food exceeds all other in immediate importance. We are appalled by the conditions of virtual famine under which the whole urban population – manual and intellectual workers alike – are living. A particularly serious effect of the blockade policy has been the cutting off of soap and of medical supplies. Epidemics of typhus fever and of a recurrent fever have swept over the whole county."[4]

The report concluded with the signatories making their "unanimous and wholehearted protest" against the policy "whose effects we have described". They recommended that:

> "the entire British Labour movement should demand the removal of the last vestige of blockade and intervention and the complete destruction of the barrier which imperialist States have erected between our own people and our brothers and sisters of Russia".

So strong was the response of the workers to the Hands off Russia Committee propaganda (and to the report, however moderately phrased, of the Labour delegation) that the supporters of the government thought it necessary to smooth things down. To counteract the effect of the propaganda carried in the *Daily Herald*, as well as in the weekly socialist papers which were not merely defending the Soviet Union but expressing out-and-out propaganda for revolution in Britain, numerous articles began to be written explaining that the British Government's intentions were pure and concerned only with the early securing of peace and good relations with the people of the Soviet Union.

But hardly had June 1920 ended when at the beginning of July there appeared in the *Daily Herald* the publication of the Golovin Papers.

2   The Golovin Papers

Lt-Gen Golovin a year earlier had been the official representative of Admiral Kolchak, General Denikin and the other White Russian armies. Various Tsarist officials in Paris were linked up with them, such as Sazonov, the former Tsarist Minister of Foreign Affairs, and the terrorist Boris Savinkov. These in May 1919 were in very close contact with the Secretary of State for War, Winston Churchill. On May 5, 1919, there was a meeting of Lt-Gen Golovin and Churchill. In the report which the ex-Tsarist general submitted to his superiors he told what had happened at that interview. Unfortunately for him the secret archives of the White Guard Government in Murmansk were captured by the Red Army and the papers were transmitted to the *Daily Herald*. From these papers it appeared that at half past 5 in the afternoon of May 15, 1919, in the interview with General Golovin, Churchill had been very much incensed at the opposition of British working men and of some Liberals to the intervention in Soviet Russia. Churchill hoped to send an additional 10,000 "volunteers" for the campaign in northern Russia. Serious demoralisation, he knew, had set in amongst British and American troops there and reinforcements were badly needed. Churchill had also stressed his anxiety to assist General Denikin. He proposed to help Denikin with 2,500 "volunteers" for service as military instructors and technical experts. As for immediate material help, the general was told £24 million would be allocated immediately. Further, there would be equipment and arms for the 100,000 troops of General Yudenich who would then march along the Gulf of Finland upon Petrograd. Further arrangements would be made for 500 Tsarist officers, at that moment prisoners-of-war in Germany, to be taken to Archangelsk at Britain's expense. Golovin concluded:

> "The result of the interview exceeded all my expectations. Churchill is not only a sympathiser but an energetic and active friend. The greatest possible aid is assured us. Now we have to show the English that we are ready to turn words into deeds."

It was a nail in the coffin of Churchill's continued frenzied endeavours when the *Daily Herald* produced this report. The effect of it was to cast deep doubt upon the sincerity of the British Government and the British Cabinet in which Churchill was such an active and influential member.

3   The Polish War

In the course of the negotiations and at the point where a trading agreement or the clauses thereof had been agreed in London and accepted in Moscow, Great Britain suddenly, on July 11, had brought in a new stipulation. This was designed to help their friends, the Poles, who were beginning to lose heavily in their unprovoked war on the Soviet Union, whose government had already instructed its Supreme Command to enter into pourparlers with the Poles for an armistice. Negotiations were to begin on August 1.

When the delegates met on the night of August 1, it turned out that the Polish delegates had no powers to fix preliminary peace terms. Negotiations broke down. The British Government now intervened. They demanded that the Russian advance stop, failing which, Lord Curzon said in his Note of August 3 – and Lloyd George stressed it in his interview with Kamenev and Krassin on August 4 – military aid would immediately be given to Poland. Meanwhile newspapers began to report British military and naval preparations. British troops were being used at Danzig to unload supplies to Poland. On Friday, August 6, a British memorandum was sent to Moscow demanding a 10-day truce under threat of what they would do if this was not obeyed. Meanwhile however the Poles had decided to accept the Russian proposals for negotiation and the Russians, on the 7th, arranged for a meeting at Minsk 4 days later. An Anglo-French Conference was held at Hythe on August 8, whereupon the Russian reply was treated as a rejection. The Anglo-French threat would now be put into force. The matter was referred to the military and naval staff to prepare for action. This put the fat in the fire.

On that weekend of August 8 and 9 much was to happen.

Once more the country was on the brink of war. On Friday, August 7, *The Times* stated:

"It is a terrible truth that once more we stand upon the edge of a crisis fraught with possibilities only less tragic than those that lowered over us in this first week of August six years ago."

This sentence meant war.

That same day, August 7, 1920, Arthur Henderson, then on his sick-bed, took action as secretary of the Labour Party. He sent a telegram to every local Labour Party in the country in the following terms:

> "Extremely menacing possibility extension Polish-Russian war. Strongly urge local parties immediately organise citizen demonstrations against intervention and supply men and munitions to Poland. Demand peace negotiations, immediate raising blockade, resumption trade relations. Send resolutions Premier and Press. Deputise local MP."[5]

At the same time the newly-formed Communist Party of Great Britain sent telegrams to Party branches in 30 chief industrial centres urging, among other things, the formation of "action committees", followed by an advertisement in the form of a manifesto in the *Daily Herald* special edition on Sunday August 9.

The response was unexampled. Huge demonstrations were held throughout the country at which resolutions were enthusiastically carried demanding peace, and protesting against any declaration of war upon the Soviets. On Sunday August 9 the Council of Action was formed by a joint meeting of the Parliamentary Committee of the Trades Union Congress, the Labour Party and the Parliamentary Labour Party. This joint meeting declared for "direct action", that is, for strikes in the event of the Polish war being further supported by Britain. Next day, the Council of Action thus formed went on a deputation to the Prime Minister. At the same time the matter was raised with the utmost urgency by Labour and Liberal MPs in Parliament. Arthur Henderson had at the right moment sounded a call which found an echo through the whole of the working class and indeed also throughout the minds and feelings of the British petty bourgeoisie.

A national Labour Conference was summoned at short notice and met on Friday August 13. Unanimously the delegates decided for a general strike to enforce peace and to protect the Soviet Union. They widened the call and asked for the formation of local Councils of Action; this was on August 15. Already many of these had been formed throughout the country. In mid-August Councils of Action were being brought into existence. Such Councils of Action had never been formed before in Britain and they were regarded for a little while as being in some way the equivalent of the Soviets that had been formed in March 1917 throughout Russia. They marked the high point of the growing movement since November 1918 for 'Hands off Russia', for peace and friendship with the Russian people and against all the plans and plots of the capitalists to put an end to Bolshevism.

The British Government saw the red light at once, and Lloyd George immediately made a pacific declaration only 48 hours after it had been announced that the dogs of war were being let loose. It was, however, left to the French ally to carry out what had been up to that point the joint policy of the two governments.

On August 9, 1920, the National Council of Action had been formed; on Tuesday, Lloyd George declared in the House of Commons they had decided to await the outcome of the Minsk negotiations between the Russians and the Poles and that there would be "intervention only if the independence of Poland was threatened". That same night, August 10, the Soviet representatives in London issued a summary of Russia's peace terms to Poland. In these terms Russia recognised the independence of Poland with a frontier more generous than that proposed by the Allies, and it called for:(1) reduction of the Polish army to 60,000 with a civic militia; (2) the demobilisation of war industries and the exclusion of war materials or troops from Britain, France or other countries; (3) unrestricted commercial transit through Poland to the Baltic. The fourth Russian point was that land should be given to the dependants of Polish soldiers who had been killed or incapacitated in the war brought on their country by the folly and wickedness of Pilsudski and his British and French Allies. All this brought a prospect of peace.

The prospects of peace raised in this manner, however, were dispersed again by a curious succession of events. On the day following Lloyd George's pacific statement the French Government issued an official recognition of Wrangel, the successor of Denikin in South Russia. Wrangel's forces had previously been saved from destruction by Lord Curzon's appeal to the Russian Government in the name of humanity. In the meantime Wrangel had taken the opportunity of these negotiations to re-equip himself with British supplies and to enter on a fresh offensive. This, and the recognition of him by the French Government, was tantamount to a new declaration of war. The French Government, on behalf of its own ruling class and, to some extent, on behalf of the British ruling class, whose direct efforts had been completely checked by the Councils of Action with their threat of direct nationwide strikes which could have paralysed the British economy and brought down the government, was now forwarding supplies and munitions and officers into Poland.

With the peace between Poland and Russia, the peace of Riga, the war on the western front came to an end. On the southern front the storming of Perikop and the capture of Sebastopol put an end, in November 1920, to General Wrangel. The last invaders and the last White Guard troops had been cleared out of European Russia. In this the effort of the Russian people, workers and peasants, had been decisive. But a part had been played by the British workers in their trade unions and socialist parties joining together in the Councils of Action.

Until the autumn of 1920 and the early winter was over the Councils of Action remained vigilant. One result of this was that, in spite of the pressure of the reactionaries inside the government and in Parliament, and in spite of all the spokesmen of the bond-holders, the war was not renewed. Nevertheless there were hankerings after the past in government departments of the British Ministry. Gradually, however, with the consciousness of the vigilance of the Labour movement, one forward step after another was taken. An exchange of prisoners began and was slowly carried out from early winter of 1920 onwards. A draft agreement was drawn up in November and met with the denunciation of the leading capitalist papers and of such bodies as the British Chambers of Commerce. For example:

> "[T]he Council of the Association of the British Chambers of Commerce, respectfully inform His Majesty's Government that no agreement between the British Government and the Russian Authorities can be supported by the representatives of British commerce and industry unless it provides for the recognition by Russia of all pre-war Russian debts, national, municipal and private."[6]

Finally, however, in the New Year 1921, on January 11, Krassin left London with a draft trading agreement. In this there were such details as:

(1) that it was preliminary to a treaty of peace;
(2) that it dealt for the moment only with trade;
(3) that neither country was to carry out propaganda against the other.

There were, however, still some snags. These were swept away as the result of an awkward incident. On February 28, 1921, the *Daily Herald* published a photograph of a copy of a forged edition of *Pravda* printed in London. It was an endeavour to stimulate trouble inside the Soviet Union. This bogus *Pravda* had been printed by a London firm and had, according to the law, the imprint on the back page. The Special Branch of Scotland Yard had taken the papers and, in their secret printing press, cut off the tell-tale imprint with their guillotine. Could it be true? Surely impossible. But it was true; it was so admitted in the House of Commons on March 3, 1921. It meant that while the Board of Trade and Foreign Office were negotiating, officials of the Home Office, Admiralty and Foreign Office, acting clandestinely, were endeavouring to foment civil war amongst the Soviet people. They were transmitting these forged *Pravdas*, of which there had been a series, through the Special Branch of Scotland Yard to certain British officials, and these officials were handing them over to White Guards, by whom they were to be smuggled into Soviet Russia.

The Councils of Action were, of course, not the work of a day or a week. The campaign for 'Hands off Russia' had reached a high point and attained a most significant success. Henceforth the danger of war had been driven away for a good long time to come.

The impact of the Russian Revolution upon the working people of Britain had resulted, after the tribulation of the war period and the revolutionary year 1919, in an astounding high pitch of demonstrations of solidarity and aid to the Soviet Union.

Notes and References

1   Passed simultaneously at the same meeting was a resolution on the Amritsar Massacre as follows: "That the action of the British general at Amritsar in causing his troops to surround and massacre a helpless and unarmed crowd of Hindu men and women assembled in orderly meeting is Prussianism of the type which our young men died to abolish. It will seriously impair the prestige of the British nation and calls for immediate drastic punishment of all implicated, and stern repudiation of their action by the British Government." [For this and the Ireland/Poland resolution see R Page Arnot, *The Miners: Years of Struggle*, George Allen & Unwin, London, 1953, pp 228-9 –*Ed.*]

2   See *Ibid*, p 229 –*Ed.*

3   They included: Robert Smillie, president of the Miners' Federation of Great Britain; Tom Mann, general secretary, Amalgamated Society of Engineers; John Bromley, general secretary, Associated Society of Locomotive Engineers and Firemen; A G Cameron, general secretary, Amalgamated Society of Carpenters and Joiners; Alex Gossip, general secretary, Furnishing Trades Association.

4   See W P and Z Coates, *A History of Anglo-Soviet Relations*, Lawrence & Wishart, 1943, pp 28-29 –*Ed.*

5   See *Ibid*, p 42 –*Ed.*

6   See *Ibid*, p 45 –*Ed.*

9 The Final Impact

I   A party of a new type

Together with the high tide reached by the trade union and Labour organisations of Britain in the formation of the Councils of Action in August 1920 against the threat of war, the impact of the Russian Revolution reached a climax for the time being in its effect on the political organisations themselves. The effect both of the Revolution and the crisis caused by counter-revolution was seen in the Councils of Action and the postures adopted by the Labour Party and trade union leaders in response to the groundswell of anti-war feeling, not only amongst the working class but throughout the petty bourgeoisie of Great Britain, when "the nation of shopkeepers" as well as the proletariat was roused. But there was also an effect upon the socialist parties as well as upon the Labour Party. The Revolution brought them together and reinvigorated them. The culminating effect was in August 1920 when one main party, the British Socialist Party, and numerous sections, minorities, committees and groupings came together to form the Communist Party of Great Britain.

To understand this delayed effect it is necessary to go back to the opening weeks of the Revolution in Russia when Lenin's *April Theses* became the Bolshevik policy and even further back to the fight against war within the Socialist International.

Just before that spring of 1917 what did the world look like? What were the prospects for its future? To a neutral but highly interested onlooker, say in the Scandinavian countries, the prospect seemed bleak enough. Here was the continent of Europe, a highly developed civilisation, whose constituent parts were locked in deadly combat, tearing one another to pieces. More than that, it looked as though the war would never end, while it, step by step, was spreading into other continents involving all but a very few countries. It was to be the First World War.

In that bitter January and February of 1917 there did not appear any immediate ray of hope. No-one knew what the end would be except more and more slaughter, more privation, starvation and famine, more worsening of conditions in every country. As Lenin wrote in the book he was then compiling on *The State and Revolution:*

> "The unheard-of horrors and miseries of the protracted war are making the position of the masses unbearable and increasing their indignation."[1]

Let us for a moment take an observer in neutral Switzerland, more neutral than the Scandinavian countries, in which Sweden was as obviously and notoriously pro-German as Norway was practically a portion of the Allied camp. To Lenin, in Switzerland, things presented an entirely different aspect. Others saw the picture of a European continent of high civilisation with all its works of peace catastrophically, accidentally and, as it were, preternaturally interrupted by the ancient God of War, Mars in his full armour, an almost unbelievable catastrophe and never likely to be repeated, so that in country after country it had become fashionable to quote the slogan, 'The War to End War'. To Lenin the aspect was totally different. For him imperialism and war, ruling class and working class, were parts of one single whole. The war, so far from being an accident, was an inevitable outcome of the free enterprise society of Europe in its latest stage, the stage of monopoly capitalism, of imperialism, defined by him a year earlier as having economic and political features whose interplay had been driving the dozen great powers of the world toward this horrible convict. It was an imperialist war proceeding from monopoly capitalism where the ruling class had become a finance oligarchy, oppressing subject nations and exploiting the working class both at home and abroad. He saw too the organisations of the working class rotted with opportunism or misled by opportunist leaders so that the topmost organisation of all, the International Socialist Bureau, had completely failed the workers. The collapse of the Socialist International, which had been the hope of the world, expressed in the song of thirty years earlier, "The Internationale shall be the Human race" – this too, he saw, and the reasons for it, in the enrichment of upper strata of the working class in the European countries at the expense of many more millions exploited in the colonies. Just as war had been the inevitable product of capitalism in its latest stage, so to Lenin there was one necessary and inevitable answer. It was to utilise the crisis arising from the war to get rid of the class rule of the bourgeoisie and to substitute for it directly the class rule of the proletariat. Once the proletariat was in control of society as a whole, controlling all its economic and financial activities, then questions of nationalisation and the series of steps towards socialism and common ownership, common administration, could be tackled steadily one by one. The essential prerequisite was to get rid of the ruling class and to have the working class in control. Very few had been alert to carry out the policy of socialism as laid down in the International Socialist Congresses in the resolutions on war for the 25 years of the Second International. Lenin saw it as his business to find the precise way in which these policies forsaken by the majority could now be implemented. Yet there was very little sign of hope on the horizon during that bitter January of 1917. Only a matter of weeks before March 12, Lenin had said in a lecture to a local Swiss organisation:

> "We of the older generation may not live to see the decisive battles of this coming revolution."[2]

Yet it was at this moment, in proverbial phrase, 'the darkest hour before the dawn', that Lenin, as we can see from all his writings, public and private, and indeed throughout the whole of the 30 months since August 1914, had reached conclusions which, immediately the Revolution began in Russia, could be formulated by him in the *Letters from Afar*[3] and finally set down in *The April Theses*.

2 The Tenth Thesis

Within a year these ten theses were so far on the way to fulfilment that they might be regarded not so much as a programme to be argued for and, as we know, to become finally successful within the ranks of the Bolshevik Party, but as a prophecy, a prediction based on a startling insight and a profound and correct deep-going analysis not only of the Russian, but of the whole world situation. From the acceptance of the *April Theses* by the Bolshevik Conference in May 1917 it was only 6 months to the victory of the October Revolution. Then, from November 1917 onward, week by week, and month by month, all the items, whether explicitly set forth or implicit in the whole body of programmes and experience for the past 15 years of the Bolshevik Party, were one by one put into operation. Against incredible odds, against every sort of provocation, against weak-mindedness, rashness, obstinacy, vainglory, sloth, self-conceit and sometimes plain obstinate stupidity even amongst the leaders of the Bolshevik Party itself, Lenin carried through the programme outlined in the Theses. It became clear that every one of them, given normal conditions of revolutionary development, would presently be fulfilled. Seldom did it seem that a prophecy so completely disbelieved in at the beginning of the year could be so completely carried through within that year itself.

But there were not to be any "normal conditions" of revolutionary development. First came the attempt of the German enemy to enforce the peace of Brest-Litovsk (the Tilsit peace) and thereafter to cut off the Bolsheviks from the Ukraine, a crippling circumstance that lasted over 6 months. But only 3 of these 6 months had elapsed when intervention by the former Allies was launched and was not to cease for the astonishingly long period of 3 years.

The infamous Cordon Sanitaire, the tight encirclement, the blanket of the dark, the closing down of news, the blockade, the shutting within a steel circle of hostile guns and bayonets; all these things cut off direct communication between the workers and peasants of Russia and the workers and peasants of the countries of Europe and further afield. Consequently one of the stipulations of the *April Theses* (No 10) could not be immediately fulfilled, namely:

> "A new international. We must take the initiative of creating a revolutionary international, an international directed against the *Social-Chauvinists*, and against the 'Centre'."

This could not be created while there was still no communication between those who had remained, like Lenin, true to the teachings of socialism, and had tried to carry out, at any rate within their means, the instructions of the Basle Resolution, the instruction of the last of 3 congresses of the old Socialist International. Fulfilment of the Tenth Thesis had to be put off from month to month.

3 The revolutionary spirit of Europe

Then came the Armistice in November 1918 and the instructions to the Germans immediately as to how to retire or not retire from the Bolshevik borders.[4]

Meantime, before the Tenth Thesis could be carried out, the Armistice with Germany had been signed on November 11, 1918. Even while preparations were being made for signature there had been response to the Soviet appeal. In some cities of Germany strikes broke out and there was the formation of what appeared to be Soviets, that is, councils of representatives of the workers. It was the beginning of the German Revolution.

The German Revolution as it turned out was only partially successful. The first stage was carried through. Early in that November the Kaiser Wilhelm II and 23 attendant kings and princes, the King of Saxony, the King of Bavaria, the King of Württemburg and a score of others had all hastily vacated their thrones and made for the nearest safe place. The Kaiser, who was to have been hanged by the Allies, as the Nazi leaders were afterwards hanged at Nuremberg in 1946, found political asylum in the Netherlands. He was to remain happily in his private castle of Doom in Holland until the eve of the Second World War.

But it was not only Workers' and Soldiers' Councils that were formed by the workers, soldiers and sailors of Germany. The League of Spartacus headed by Rosa Luxemburg, Karl Liebkneckt and Franz Mehring had transformed itself into the Communist Party of Germany. This was intended to be an example of the fast-working mole of history.[5] On January 5, 1919, there were 'Spartacus riots' in Berlin; and the Bolsheviks, having occupied Riga on January 2, 1919, were approaching East Prussia by January 11. The 'Spartacus' rising was crushed on January 13 in Berlin and on January 15 Karl Liebknecht and Rosa Luxemburg were murdered.

Nevertheless in every country, victor or vanquished, the disturbances continued. In Britain there were over 50 mutinies of the army in the one month of January 1919. Before the end of March a Soviet government under Bela Kun was established in Hungary; and by the beginning of April the Bavarian Soviet Government was set up in Bavaria. Consequently, as it seemed, in 1919 the crisis created by the war was developing; and certainly the class consciousness of the workers was rising to hitherto untouched and unattained heights. It was in the beginning of March in semi-starved and completely encircled Moscow, that there was called the First Congress of a new International. It was the implementation at last of the Tenth Thesis.

4 The Communist International

The First Congress of the Communist International was held in Moscow from March 2 to 19, 1919, with a small number of delegates present. Owing to the difficult circumstances of the blockade the delegations to the First Congress, as sorted out by Chicherin, who was in charge of the credentials commission, numbered only 19:

and of these over half came from distinct nationalities within what had once been the Russian Empire. The delegates of the other 9 countries were those who, through nearness to the beleaguered Soviet Union, had somehow managed to get across the closely guarded frontiers, from Germany, Austria, Hungary, the Balkans and Scandinavia. The main thesis presented was that by Lenin on "Bourgeois Democracy and Proletarian Dictatorship". The resolutions adopted the thesis. The Manifesto of the Communist International "to the workers of all lands", issued two years after the first stage of the Russian Revolution in Petrograd, was a stirring utterance, beginning with the words:

> "Seventy-two years have gone by since the Communist Party proclaimed its programme in the form of the Manifesto written by the greatest teachers of the proletarian revolution, Karl Marx and Friedrich Engels. Even at that early time, when Communism had scarcely come into the arena of conflict, it was pursued by the lies, hatred and calumny of the possessing classes, who rightly suspected in it their mortal enemy.
>
> …
>
> "We communists, representatives of the revolutionary proletariat of the different countries of Europe and Asia and America, assembled in Soviet Moscow, feel and consider ourselves followers and fulfillers of the programme proclaimed 72 years ago.

Then in a new paragraph it said:

> "Spurning the half-heartedness, hypocrisy and corruption of the decadent official Socialist parties, we the Communists assembled in the Third International, feel ourselves to be the direct successors of the heroic efforts and martyrdom of a long series of revolutionary generations from Baboeuf to Karl Liebknecht and Rosa Luxemburg."

In the course of the programme there were concluding sentences of urgent appeal as follows:

> "As the First International foresaw future developments and pointed the way as the Second International gathered together and organised millions of the proletarians, so the Third International is the International of open mass action, of revolutionary realisation, the *International of Deeds*.
>
> "Socialist criticism has sufficiently stigmatised the bourgeois world order. The task of the International Communist Party is now to overthrow this order and to erect in its place the structure of the Socialist world order. We urge the working men and women of all countries to unite under the Communist banner,

the emblem under which the first great victories have already been won.

"Proletarians of all countries! In the war against imperialistic barbarity, against monarchy, against the privileged classes, the bourgeois State and bourgeois property, against all forms and varieties of social and national oppression – UNITE!

Under the standard of the Workers' Councils. under the banner of the Third International, in the revolutionary struggle for power and the dictatorship of the proletariat, proletarians of all countries, UNITE!"[6]

It was a stirring manifesto throughout. Hitherto appeals had been directed very largely towards the working classes of Europe and North America but this manifesto contained the phrase whose words had the sound of a mighty explosion, namely:

"Colonial slaves of Africa and Asia, when the hour of the proletarian dictatorship strikes, the hour of your liberation has come."

It was 1919. Thirty years later Asia could testify to the truth of this statement, this prediction. Ten years more and Africa could also bear witness.

5   The effect in Britain

It was not long before there were attempts made to respond to the stirring call which, in one way or another, sometimes in muted forms and sometimes fragmentarily, reached those who had sustained the burden of the struggle against the ruling classes during the war. It has already been recorded how a first attempt at a revolutionary socialist party in the last fortnight of December 1918 had not resulted in the desired unity. In 1919, however, the prospects seemed better.

Throughout 1919 and then in the early part of 1920 the British Socialist Party, which had accepted affiliation to the new Communist International by a ballot vote of the branches, was seeking to unite with the various revolutionary socialist groups in the formation of a new Communist Party. During 1919 and early 1920 various newer groupings sprang up, while some of the older bodies assumed new shapes and new programmes. There were fierce discussions about participation in Parliament, affiliation to the Labour Party and attitude to the established trade unions within both the older parties, such as the Independent Labour Party and the Socialist Labour Party, and also within the new organisations that had sprung up during the war.

The Communist Party of Great Britain, after many months of negotiations between the socialist organisations, was established at a Convention which met on July 31, 1920, in the Cannon Street Hotel (hitherto reserved almost entirely for meetings of shareholders of private capitalist companies) and on the next day in the International Socialist Club in New City Road, London.

Five months later, in January 1921, there was held the Second (Unity) Congress in Leeds at which other sections and groups, including that led by William Gallacher, also joined up together with further shop steward organisations. The Party's first activities as well as its formation had been hailed with approval by the *Daily Herald*.

Not only in the columns of the *Daily Herald* – then including in its editorial staff a considerable number of members of the newly formed Party – but throughout wide circles of workers the birth of a Communist Party was taken as a climax in the impact of the Russian Revolution upon Great Britain.

Notes and References

1   Lenin, Preface to the first edition of *The State and Revolution*, in *Collected Works*, Vol 25, p 387.

2   Lenin, Lecture on the 1905 Revolution, in Collected Works, Vol 23, p 253. The quotation is in the context of Europe being "pregnant with revolution", with the "decisive battles" arguably meaning Europe-wide –*Ed*

3   Lenin, in *Collected Works*, Vol 23, pp 295-342 –*Ed*.

4   These instructions were afterwards to be repeated in the terms of the Armistice: see Appendix to this chapter.

5   The Prince of Denmark says: "Well said, old mole! canst work i' th' earth so fast?" It was Karl Marx who adopted from Shakespeare this phrase and bestowed it upon the subterranean and invisible working of the forces, especially the class forces, of history.

6   See R P Dutt, *The Two Internationals*, Labour Research Department/George Allen & Unwin, 1920, p 68ff; online at https://archive.org/stream/twointernational00dutt/twointernational00dutt_djvu.txt –*Ed*.

Appendix

Extract from Conditions of Armistice with Germany

(SIGNED NOVEMBER 11, 1918)

(B) Clauses relating to the Eastern Frontiers of Germany
15. Annulment of the Treaties of Bucharest and Brest-Litovsk and of supplementary treaties.
16. The Allies shall have free access to the territories evacuated by the Germans on their eastern frontier, either via Danzig or by the Vistula, in order to revictual the populations of those territories or to maintain order.

(D) General Clauses
19. ... Restitution of the Russian and Rumanian gold removed by the Germans or handed over to them. This gold to be delivered in trust to the Allies until the signature of peace.

Extracts from the Treaty of Versailles

Part III, Section XIV. Russia and Russian States

Article 116.
Germany acknowledges and agrees to respect as permanent and inalienable the independence of all the territories which were part of the former Russian Empire on August 1, 1914.

In accordance with the provisions of Article 259 of Part IX (Financial Clauses) and Article 395 of Part X (Economic Clauses), Germany accepts definitely the abrogation of the Brest-Litovsk treaties and of all other treaties, conventions, and agreements entered into by her with the Maximalist Government in Russia.

The Allied and Associated Powers formally reserve the rights of Russia to obtain from Germany restitution and reparation based on the principles of the present Treaty.

Article 117.
Germany undertakes to recognise the full force of all treaties or agreements which may be entered into by the Allied and Associated Powers with States now existing or coming into existence in future in the whole or part of the former Empire of Russia as it existed on August 1, 1914, and to recognise the frontiers of any such States as determined therein.

Part XIV, Section II. Eastern Europe

Article 433.

As a guarantee for the execution of the provisions of the present treaty, by which Germany accepts definitely the abrogation of the Brest-Litovsk Treaty, and of all treaties, conventions, and agreements entered into by her with the Maximalist Government in Russia, and in order to ensure the restoration of peace and good government in the Baltic Provinces and Lithuania, all German troops at present in the said territories shall return to within the frontiers of Germany as soon as the Governments of the Principal Allied and Associated Powers shall think the moment suitable, having regard to the internal situation of these territories. These troops shall abstain from all requisitions and seizures and from any other coercive measures, with a view to obtaining supplies intended for Germany, and shall in no way interfere with such measures for national defence as may be adopted by the Provisional Governments of Estonia, Latvia, and Lithuania.

No other German troops shall, pending the evacuation or after the evacuation is complete, be admitted to the said territories.

Index of Names

Buckler, W H, 137
Bullitt, W C, 139
Bullock, Alan, 147
Burke, Edmund, 17
Burns, John, 52
Burns, Robert, 35
Byron, Lord, 35

Cade, Jack, 128
Caesar, Julius, 5
Cameron, A G, 159
Campbell-Bannerman, Sir Henry, 12
Carr, E H, 136
Carson, Sir E, 59, 101
Catherine II, Empress, 35
Cecil, Lord Robert, 59, 97, 102, 104, 146, 148
Charles I, King, 25
Chekhov, Anton, 35
Chernov, V M, 72
Chicherin, Georgy (*also* Chicherine), 30, 109, 116, 117, 123, 137, 144, 149, 150, 151
Chkheidze, N S, 19, 29, 31, 33
Churchill, Winston S, 93, 109, 125, 128, 130, 132, 133, 144, 145, 148, 154, 155
Clemenceau, Georges, 148
Coates, W P and Zelda (*also* Kahan), 5, 136, 151, 159
Cole, G D H, 1, 2, 128
Connolly, James, 128
Cromwell, Oliver, 111
Cunninghame Graham, R B, 45
Curzon, Marquess, 40, 59, 146, 149, 150, 151, 155, 157

Dan, F I, 75
Davis, Jerome, 3
De Leon, Daniel, 127
Denikin, General, 70, 124, 130, 143, 144, 146, 148, 157
Devlin, J, 18
Dukhonin, N N, 94, 95
Duncan, Charles, 31
Dutov, A I, 89, 130
Dybenko, P Y, 81
Dzherzinsky, F, 89

Edward Vll, King, 40
Eichhorn, Field Marshal von, 121
Elizabeth I, Queen, 35
Engels, F, 19, 36, 49, 164
Ewer, W N, 1, 134

Fairchild, E C, 56, 126
Farbman, M G, 12
Franz Ferdinand, Archduke, 43
Freud, Sigmund, 93
Fyfe, H H, 13

Gallacher, William, 31, 57, 103, 127, 134, 166
George V, King, 13, 146, 152
Gladstone, W E, 40
Godunev, M, 31
Golovin, Lt-General, 154, 155
Goode, Prof W T, 143, 145
Gorbounov, N, 113
Gorky, Maxim, 65, 80, 90
Gosling, Harry, 31
Gossip, Alex, 159
Grenfell, Capt Harold 143, 145
Grey, Sir Edward, 104
Guesde, Jules, 64
Guchkov, A I, 28, 31, 69

Hankey, Sir M P A, 59
Hardie, J Keir, 40, 44, 45, 51
Harmsworth, Cecil, 42
Hartshorn, Vernon, 133
Henderson, Arthur, 18, 19, 30, 40, 44, 45, 47, 48, 50, 58, 59, 60, 61, 62, 63, 111, 156
Hertling, Graf von, 105
Hill, John, 31
Hitler, Adolf, 131
Hobson, S G, 21
Hodge, John, 30, 48
Hoeglund, Z, 54
Holmes, Walter M, 1, 134